Coaching Youth
Cheerleading

American Sport Education Program

Endorsed by Varsity Brands

Human Kinetics

Library of Congress Cataloging-in-Publication Data

Coaching youth cheerleading / American Sport Education Program.
   p. cm.
 ISBN-13: 978-0-7360-7444-5 (soft cover)
 ISBN-10: 0-7360-7444-9 (soft cover)
 1. Cheerleading. I. American Sport Education Program.
 LB3635.C63 2008
 791.6'4--dc22
                          2007045409
 ISBN-10: 0-7360-7444-9 (print)
 ISBN-13: 978-0-7360-7444-5 (print)

The Web addresses cited in this text were current as of January 2009, unless otherwise noted.

Acquisitions Editors: Amy Tocco and Jenny Maddox; **Project Writers:** William Seely and Chris Darby; **Project Consultants:** Becky Gennings, Heather Seely, and Jennifer Uselton; **Developmental Editor:** Laura Floch; **Assistant Editors:** Cory Weber, Laura Koritz, and Elizabeth Watson; **Copyeditor:** Susan Campanini; **Proofreaders:** Ray Vallese and Joanna Hatzopoulos Portman; **Permission Manager:** Carly Breeding; **Graphic Designer:** Nancy Rasmus; **Graphic Artist:** Julie L. Denzer; **Cover Designer:** Keith Blomberg; **Photographer (cover):** © Varsity Brands; **Photographer (interior):** Neil Bernstein, unless otherwise noted; photos on pages 1, 9, 19, 25, 35, 39, 51, 63, 93, 105, 115 © Varsity Brands; **Photo Asset Manager:** Laura Fitch; **Visual Production Assistant:** Joyce Brumfield; **Photo Production Manager:** Jason Allen; **Art Manager:** Kelly Hendren; **Associate Art Manager**: Alan L. Wilborn; **Illustrator:** Gary Hunt; **Printer:** United Graphics

We thank Grace Evangelical Church in Germantown, Tennessee, for assistance in providing the location for the photo shoot for this book.

Copies of this book are available at special discounts for bulk purchase for sales promotions, premiums, fund-raising, or educational use. Special editions or book excerpts can also be created to specifications. For details, contact the Special Sales Manager at Human Kinetics.

Printed in the United States of America   10 9 8 7 6 5 4 3 2 1

The paper in this book is certified under a sustainable forestry program.

Human Kinetics
Web site: www.HumanKinetics.com

United States: Human Kinetics
P.O. Box 5076, Champaign, IL 61825-5076
800-747-4457
e-mail: humank@hkusa.com

Canada: Human Kinetics
475 Devonshire Road Unit 100
Windsor, ON N8Y 2L5
800-465-7301 (in Canada only)
e-mail: info@hkcanada.com

Europe: Human Kinetics
107 Bradford Road, Stanningley
Leeds LS28 6AT, United Kingdom
+44 (0) 113 255 5665
e-mail: hk@hkeurope.com

Australia: Human Kinetics
57A Price Avenue
Lower Mitcham, South Australia 5062
08 8372 0999
e-mail: info@hkaustralia.com

New Zealand: Human Kinetics
Division of Sports Distributors NZ Ltd.
P.O. Box 300 226 Albany
North Shore City, Auckland
0064 9 448 1207
e-mail: info@humankinetics.co.nz

Contents

Welcome to Coaching

Coaching young people is an exciting way to be involved in sport. However, there can be many challenges that come along with this opportunity. Although some coaches are overwhelmed by the responsibilities of helping athletes through their early athletic experiences, *Coaching Youth Cheerleading* can serve as a valuable resource to help you prepare for success in this role.

Coaching cheerleading is not just about bringing megaphones and pom poms to the field, it is about the physical and mental preparation required to perform with the highest level of safety. As a coach, you have the opportunity to serve as a positive role model and instructor to young athletes, while providing the guidance they need to excel.

Coaching Youth Cheerleading will help you meet these challenges, so that you can experience the many rewards of coaching and also provide a positive contribution to your team. Within this course of instruction, you will learn how to meet your responsibilities as a coach, communicate effectively, provide instruction for optimal safety, and teach skills while sustaining a fun environment. You will also learn strategies for season preparation and game day coaching.

This book serves as a text for ASEP's and Varsity Brands' Coaching Youth Cheerleading course. For more information about this course or any ASEP and Varsity Brands resources, please contact the following:

ASEP
P.O. Box 5076
Champaign, IL 61825-5076
800-747-5698
www.ASEP.com

Varsity Brands
6745 Lenox Center Court, Ste. 300
Memphis, TN 38115
800-238-0286
www.varsity.com

Welcome From Varsity Brands

Dear Coach:

I would like to welcome you to the exciting world of youth cheerleading! On behalf of Varsity Brands, I commend you for committing the extra time required to be a coach and for taking the initiative to learn more about this rewarding athletic activity.

Since our inception in 1974, Varsity Brands has become synonymous with cheerleading and has helped expand its popularity significantly through several educational companies, including: Universal Cheerleaders Association (UCA), National Cheerleaders Association (NCA), and our ESPN-televised national championships.

As the largest cheerleading education company in the world, our goal is to provide the best cheerleading instruction available. We are proud to partner with ASEP, the leader in educational sports publishing, to bring you this introduction to coaching youth cheerleading.

This season, you have an opportunity to build and shape the lives of young people through the relationships you develop with them as their coach. We hope that you will help us make a positive difference in their lives through the dynamic and exciting activity of cheerleading.

If you have any questions or need our assistance, please contact us at 800-238-0286. We wish you all the best with your coaching career!

Sincerely,

Jeff Webb
President and CEO
Varsity Brands

A Note About Safety From the American Association of Cheerleading Coaches and Administrators

The American Association of Cheerleading Coaches and Administrators (AACCA) is a safety organization founded in 1987. The mission of the AACCA is to increase safety measures and help minimize cheerleading injuries through education and safety rules for coaches.

The AACCA produces the *AACCA Cheerleading Safety Manual,* edited by Dr. Gerald George, with contributing experts in the fields of legal issues, medical procedures, spotting techniques, skill progressions, practice and performance environments, and other areas of risk management. This manual is the basis for the AACCA Safety Certification course given throughout the country by one of the AACCA's more than 100 safety instructors. The NCAA lists the AACCA Safety Certification course as meeting its requirement for all of its cheerleading coaches to be safety certified; several states now require the AACCA course for their cheerleading coaches at the high school level.

The AACCA conducts regional and national conventions for coaches each year in addition to offering safety courses at most state cheerleading coaches' conferences. More information and safety course dates and locations can be found at www.aacca.org.

Stepping Into Coaching

I f you are like most youth cheerleading coaches, you have probably been recruited from the ranks of concerned parents, sport enthusiasts, or community volunteers. Many coaches, both novice and veteran, have had little formal coaching instruction. In this case, the coaching assignment may be challenging. However, *Coaching Youth Cheerleading* will provide the basic tools necessary to prepare youth coaches, regardless of level of experience and preparedness, for success.

To begin, we will take a look at the responsibilities and expectations of being a coach, tips for what to do if your own child is on your squad, and five important tools for being an effective coach.

Your Responsibilities as a Coach

Coaching at any level involves much more than creating cheers, sidelines, and dances or teaching your squad members how to execute a particular partner stunt. Coaching involves accepting the tremendous responsibility you face when parents put their children in your care. As a cheerleading coach, it is your responsibility to do the following:

1. *Provide a safe physical environment.*

   Cheerleading holds inherent risks. As a coach, you are responsible for regularly inspecting practice and competition areas and equipment. To avoid injury, children need to learn safety techniques and know about emergency action plans (see chapter 4 for more information).

2. *Communicate positively.*

   You have a lot to communicate, not only with your squad members and parents, but also with the coaching staff, administrators, and others. Communicate in a positive manner to demonstrate that you have the best interests of the squad members at heart (see chapter 2 for more information).

3. *Teach the philosophy and role of a cheerleading squad.*

   Introduce the general philosophy of cheerleading and incorporate it into individual instruction (see chapter 3 for more information). You can teach much of this philosophy during practice, including how to create raving fans, build traditions, and lead a crowd effectively. This is the foundation of what cheerleading is all about, so plan to review your squad's progress in this area whenever the opportunity arises.

4. *Teach the fundamental skills of cheerleading.*

   When you are teaching the fundamental skills of cheerleading, make sure that your squad members have fun by creating a practice environment that is enjoyable, yet productive. Help your squad members improve their skills by understanding the basics (see chapters 6, 7, and 8 for more information).

5. *Direct squad members in game situations and competitions.*

   This direction includes creating an effective game plan, ensuring that the material is presented at the appropriate time in the game, and making sound tactical decisions during games (see chapter 9 for more information). Remember that cheerleading is a unique athletic activity in that its primary focus is to facilitate and build crowd support for the team on the field or court. Competing with other cheerleading squads is secondary. The focus at games is to build crowd support, but the focus at cheerleading competitions is on proper execution of routines. In either case, winning at all costs is never the focus.

6. *Help your squad members become fit and value fitness for a lifetime.*

   It is important to stress the value of being physically fit, and doing so will help your squad members participate in cheerleading safely and successfully. Encourage your squad to enjoy learning about physical fitness by making fitness activities fun and motivating!

7. *Help young people develop character.*

   Character development includes caring, learning, honesty, respect, and responsibility. These intangible qualities are no less important to teach than the skill of hitting a stunt. Teach these values to squad members by demonstrating and encouraging behaviors that express these values at all times. For example, when building a stunt, emphasize that every person within that stunt plays an important role (even if she is not the one on top).

These are your responsibilities as a coach. Provide a positive learning environment in which every squad member has the opportunity to participate in the activity without fear while having fun and enjoying the entire cheerleading experience.

Coaching Your Own Child

Coaching can become even more complicated when your own child is on the squad you coach. Many coaches are parents, but the two roles should not be confused. As a parent, you are responsible for your own children, but as a coach, you are also responsible for the entire cheerleading organization, including all of the squad members and their parents. Because of this additional responsibility, your behavior as a coach is different from your behavior at home, and your daughter may not understand why.

Coaching Tip

It's important to discuss your interest in coaching cheerleading with your child before making a decision. If she has strong reservations about your taking over the head coaching job, consider becoming involved in a smaller role instead, such as being an assistant coach or organizing a group of parents who provide drinks and snacks at practices, games, and competitions.

For example, imagine the confusion of a young girl who is the center of her parents' attention at home but is barely noticed by her father (who is the coach) in the sport setting. Or consider the mixed signals received by a young squad member whose skill is constantly evaluated by the coach (who is also a mother who otherwise rarely comments on her daughter's activities). Explain your new responsibilities to your child and how they affect your relationship when you are coaching. Take the following steps to avoid problems when coaching your own child:

• Ask your child if she wants you to coach the squad.

• Explain why you want to be involved with the squad.

• Discuss with your child how your interactions change when you take on the role of coach at practices, games, or competitions.

• Limit your coaching behavior to the coaching role.

• Avoid parenting during practice, game, or competition situations to keep your role clear in your child's mind.

• Reaffirm your love for your child, regardless of her performance on the sideline or the competition mat.

Five Tools of an Effective Coach

Have you purchased the traditional coaching tools—notebook, coaching clothes, sport shoes, and a stereo? These items certainly help in the act of coaching, but to be successful, you'll need five other tools that can't be purchased. These tools are available only through self-examination and hard work. Remember them with the acronym COACH:

C	Comprehension
O	Outlook
A	Affection
C	Character
H	Humor

Comprehension

Comprehension of both the rules and skills of cheerleading is required to be successful. To improve your comprehension of cheerleading, take the following steps:

- Read about the cheerleading safety guidelines in chapter 3 of this book.
- Read about the fundamental skills of cheerleading in chapters 6-8.
- Read additional cheerleading coaching books, including those available from the American Sport Education Program (ASEP), the American Association of Cheerleading Coaches and Administrators (AACCA), and Varsity Spirit.
- Contact youth cheerleading organizations, such as Varsity Spirit.
- Attend cheerleading coaching clinics.
- Talk with more experienced coaches.
- Observe local college, high school, and youth sporting events and cheerleading competitions.
- Watch sporting events and cheerleading competitions on television.

Coaching Tip

Local college and high school football or basketball games and cheerleading competitions are a low-cost way not only for you to improve your knowledge of cheerleading but also to allow squad members of all ages to see the skills they're working on in action. Consider working with your squad members' parents to organize an outing to a local competition in place of an after-school or weekend practice.

As a coach, you need to know how to implement proper training and safety methods so that your squad members can participate with little risk of injury. Even then, accidents can occur, and you'll probably be the first person responding to your squad members' injuries. Be sure that you understand the basic emergency care procedures described in chapter 4.

Outlook

The second coaching tool refers to your perspective and goals—what you seek as a coach. The most common coaching objective is to help squad members develop their physical, mental, and social skills in a fun and dynamic environment. Thus, your outlook involves your priorities, your planning, and your vision for the future. See "Assessing Your Priorities" to learn more about the priorities that you set for yourself as a coach.

Assessing Your Priorities

Even though most coaches tend to focus on the technical aspects of cheerleading (such as stunts, motions, and dance—the attributes judged in competition), you should focus on the primary role of your squad: *building positive team spirit*. Keep the role of competition in perspective by making decisions that are in line with the primary purpose of a cheerleading squad and in the best interest of the squad members. Remember, the competitions are a secondary focus.

So, how do you know if your outlook and priorities are in order? Here's a little test:

1. Which situation would you be most proud of?

   a. *Knowing that each participant enjoyed cheering for her team.*

   b. *Seeing that all squad members improved their cheerleading skills.*

   c. *Winning the youth cheerleading championship.*

2. Which statement best reflects your thoughts about athletic activities?

   a. *If it isn't fun, don't do it.*

   b. *Everyone should learn something every day.*

   c. *Sport isn't fun if you don't win.*

3. How would you like your squad members to remember you?

   a. *As a coach who made practice and games fun.*

   b. *As a coach who provided a basic understanding of the important role of cheerleaders and fundamental cheerleading skills.*

   c. *As a coach whose squad won a lot of cheerleading competitions.*

4. Which would you most like to hear from a squad member's parent?

   a. *Nicole really had a good time cheering this year.*

   b. *Nicole learned some important lessons cheering this year.*

   c. *Nicole competed on the championship squad this year.*

5. Which of the following would be the most rewarding moment of your season?

   a. *Having your squad want to continue cheering, even after the season has come to an end.*

   b. *Seeing one of your squad members finally master the skill of an elevator.*

   c. *Winning the cheerleading championship.*

Look over your answers. If you most often selected "a" responses, having fun is most important to you. A majority of "b" answers suggests that developing the squad members themselves is what attracts you to coaching. And if "c" was your most frequent response, winning is the top on your list of coaching priorities. If your priorities are in order, your squad members' well-being takes precedence over your competition results.

ASEP has a motto that will help you keep your outlook in line with the best interests of your squad members. It summarizes in four words all you need to remember when establishing your coaching priorities:

Athletes first, winning second.

This motto recognizes that striving to win is an important, even vital, part of athletics. However, it also states that no effort to win should be made at the expense of the squad members' well-being, development, and enjoyment. Take the following actions to better define your outlook:

- With your assistant coaches, determine your priorities for the season.
- Prepare for situations that challenge your priorities.
- Set goals for yourself and your squad members that are consistent with your priorities.
- Plan how you and your squad members can best attain your goals.
- Review your goals frequently to stay on track.

Affection

Another vital tool to have in your coaching kit is a genuine concern for the young people whom you coach. This requires having a passion for kids, a desire to share your enjoyment and knowledge of cheerleading with them, and the patience and understanding that allows each squad member to grow from her involvement in athletics. You can demonstrate your affection and patience in many ways:

- Make an effort to get to know each squad member.
- Treat each squad member as an individual.
- Empathize with squad members who are trying to learn new and challenging skills.
- Treat your squad as you would like to be treated under similar circumstances.
- Control your emotions.
- Show your enthusiasm for being involved with your squad.
- Keep an upbeat tempo and a positive tone in all of your communications.

Character

The fact that you have decided to coach cheerleading probably means that you think participation in athletics is important. But whether or not that participation develops character in your squad members depends as much on you as it does on the activity itself. How can you help your squad build character?

Having good character means modeling appropriate behaviors for athletics and life. That means more than just saying the right things. What you say and what you do must match. There is no place in coaching for the "Do as I say, not as I do" philosophy. Challenge, support, encourage, and reward every youngster, and your squad members will be more likely to accept and even celebrate their differences. Be in control before, during, and after all practices, games, and competitions. Also, don't be afraid to admit when you are wrong. No one is perfect!

Each member of your coaching staff should consider the following steps to becoming a good role model:

- Take stock of your strengths and weaknesses.
- Build on your strengths.
- Refrain from actions and activities that you do not want to see copied.
- If you slip up, apologize to your squad and yourself.

Coaching Tip

Younger squad members in particular are often nervous about meeting new people and starting a new activity. A good way to break the ice with younger age groups is to tell a joke at the beginning of the first few practices. Here is an old standby:

Q: Why did it get really hot after the football game?
A: All the fans went home!

Humor

Humor is an often-overlooked coaching tool. For our purposes, humor means having the ability to laugh at yourself and with your squad during practices, games, and competitions. Nothing helps balance the seriousness of a practice session like a chuckle or two. And a sense of humor puts in perspective the many mistakes your squad members will make. So don't get upset over each miscue or respond negatively to errors. Allow yourself and your squad members to enjoy the ups without dwelling on the downs. Here are some tips for injecting humor into your practices:

- Make practices fun by including a variety of activities.
- Keep all squad members involved in skill practices and drills.
- Consider laughter by your squad members a sign of enjoyment, not disruption or lack of discipline.
- Smile!

Communicating
as a Coach

In chapter 1, you learned about the tools needed for coaching: comprehension, outlook, affection, character, and humor. These are essential for effective coaching. Without them, you'd have a difficult time getting started. However, these tools will not work if you don't know how to effectively apply them when working with your squad. This chapter examines what communication is, and how you can become a more effective communicator.

You might mistakenly believe that communication occurs only when you are instructing squad members to do something, but verbal commands are only a small part of the communication process. At least half of communication is nonverbal. When you are coaching, remember that actions speak louder than words.

Communication in its simplest form involves two people: a sender and a receiver. The sender transmits the message verbally through facial expressions, and possibly through the use of body language. Once the message is sent, the receiver receives it, and ideally understands it. A receiver who fails to attentively listen might miss part, if not all, of the message.

Sending Effective Messages

Young squad members need accurate, understandable, and supportive messages to help them learn the basics of cheerleading. This will help them as they develop skills and confidence in their own abilities. That's why your verbal and nonverbal messages are important.

Verbal Messages

The well-worn statement "Sticks and stones may break my bones, but words will never hurt me" just isn't true. Spoken words can have a strong and long-lasting effect on young athletes. Your words are particularly influential because youngsters place great importance on what their coaches say. Perhaps you don't remember much of what your elementary school teachers told you, but you may still recall specific statements your coaches made. Such is the lasting effect of a coach's comments.

Whether you are correcting misbehavior or praising a squad member for good effort, you should consider a number of factors when sending verbal messages:

- Be positive and honest.
- Speak clearly and simply.
- Say it loud enough and then say it again.
- Be consistent.

Be Positive and Honest

Nothing turns people off like hearing someone nag all the time, and children react similarly to a coach who gripes constantly. Kids need special encouragement, because they often doubt their ability to perform well in an athletic event. When possible, look for what your squad members do well and praise them for it. On the other hand, don't cover up poor or incorrect technique with words of praise. Kids know all too well when they've made an error, and no cheerfully expressed cliché can undo their mistakes.

An effective way to correct a performance error is to first point out the part of the skill or behavior that the squad member performed correctly. Next, explain in a positive manner the error that she made and demonstrate how to perform the skill the correct way. Finish by encouraging her and emphasizing correct performance.

Make sure you don't follow a positive statement with the word *but*. For example, don't say, "Way to step and lock, Melissa, but if you push down through the bases' shoulders more, you'll pop up much quicker." Many kids ignore the positive statement and focus on the negative one. Instead, say, "Great job of stepping and locking, Melissa. And if you push down through your bases' shoulders a little more, you'll pop up even quicker next time. Way to go!"

Speak Clearly and Simply

Positive and honest messages are good, but only if they are expressed directly in words that your squad members can understand. If you ramble, your squad members will miss the point of your message and subsequently lose interest. Here are tips for saying things clearly:

- Organize your thoughts before speaking to your squad members.
- Know your subject as completely as possible.
- Explain things thoroughly, but don't bore your squad members with long-winded monologues.
- Use language that your squad members can understand, and be consistent in your terminology.

Say It Loud Enough and Then Say It Again

Talk to your squad members in a voice that everyone can hear. A crisp, vigorous voice commands attention and respect. They might tune out weak speech. When you are speaking to a young squad member individually about a personal problem, it's appropriate to soften your voice. But, most of the time, your messages are for all of your squad members to hear, so make sure that they can! An enthusiastic voice also motivates squad members and tells them that you enjoy being their coach. Use caution; however, avoid dominating the setting with a booming voice that takes attention away from your squad members' performances.

Coaching Tip

Terms that you are familiar with and understand might be completely foreign to your squad members, especially younger members or beginners. Adjust your vocabulary to match the age group. Although 12- to14-year-olds may understand terms such as "tighten up" or "sharper," 8- and 9-year-olds may be confused by this terminology. In many cases, you may want to use physical demonstrations with your squad members so that they can "see" the term and how it relates to cheerleading.

Sometimes what you say, even if it is stated loudly and clearly, won't sink in the first time. This may be particularly true when young squad members hear words that they don't understand. To avoid boring repetition, say the same thing in a slightly different way. For instance, if you are working on a game cheer and a few squad members are not hitting their motions on the right count, you might first say, "Okay, hit your motions on the correct word!" If they don't appear to understand, then you might say, "We have motions so the crowd knows when to yell, so it's important that we hit our motions on the key words of the cheer!" The second form of the message may get through to squad members who missed it the first time around.

Be Consistent

People often say things in ways that imply a different message. For example, a touch of sarcasm added to "Way to go!" sends an entirely different message than the words themselves suggest. Avoid sending mixed messages. Keep the tone of your voice consistent with the words that you use. Don't say something one day and then contradict it the next day; this will be very confusing to young squad members.

Also, keep your terminology consistent. Many cheerleading terms describe the same or similar skills. Take the person going on top of a stunt, for example. One coach might use the term "top person" or "top" to indicate the squad member who is going on top of a stunt, but another coach might say "flier." Although both terms are correct, to be consistent, have the staff agree on all terms before the start of the season, and then stick with those terms.

Nonverbal Messages

Just as you should be consistent in the tone of voice and words you use, you should also keep your verbal and nonverbal messages consistent. An extreme example of this kind of inconsistency is shaking your head, indicating disapproval, while saying, "Nice try." Which message should the squad member believe—your gesture or your words?

Messages can be sent nonverbally in several ways. Facial expressions and body language are just two of the more obvious forms of nonverbal signals that can help in coaching. As a coach, you need to be a teacher first. Avoid any action that detracts from the message you are trying to convey.

Facial Expressions

The look on a person's face is the quickest clue to what he or she is thinking. Your squad members know this and study your face for a sign that tells them more than the words you say. Don't try to fool them by putting on a happy or blank "mask." They'll see through it, and you'll lose credibility.

Serious, stone-faced expressions provide no cues to kids who want to know how they are performing. Don't be afraid to smile! Your smile can give a great boost to a squad member who is unsure of herself. Plus, a smile lets your squad members know that you're happy to be coaching them.

Body Language

What would your squad members think you were feeling if you came to practice slouched over, with your head down and your shoulders slumped? Would they conclude that you were tired, bored, or unhappy? What if you watched them during a game or competition with your hands on your hips, your jaws clenched, and your face reddened? Would they decide that you were upset with them, disgusted at a call on the field, or mad at a fan? Most likely, some or all of these possibilities would enter your squad members' minds. This is not the

> **Coaching Tip**
> As a coach, always be aware of your body language. Squad members of all ages pick up on your actions and habits, so provide a good example for them to model. All it takes is a few rolls of the eyes or wild hand gestures to send the message that a particular behavior is unacceptable, even if that was not your intent.

impression you want your squad members to have of you. That's why you should carry yourself in a pleasant, confident, and vigorous manner.

Physical contact can also be an important use of body language. A high five, a pat on the head, an arm around the shoulder, or even a big hug are effective ways to show approval, concern, affection, and joy to your squad members. Youngsters especially need this type of nonverbal message. Of course, keep within obvious moral and legal limits, but don't be reluctant to show positive affection toward your team.

Improving Receiving Skills

What about the other half of the communication process: *receiving* messages? Too often, good senders of messages are poor receivers. As a coach, you need to fulfill both roles effectively.

The requirements for receiving messages are simple, but receiving skills are perhaps less satisfying, and therefore underdeveloped compared with sending skills. People seem to enjoy hearing themselves talk more than they enjoy hearing others talk. If you learn the keys to receiving messages and make a strong effort to use them with your squad members, you'll be surprised by what you've been missing.

Pay Attention

First, pay attention. Hear what others need as they communicate with you. That's not always easy when you're busy coaching and have many things competing for your attention. But, in one-on-one or group meetings with squad members, focus on what they are telling you, both verbally and nonverbally. You'll be amazed at the little signals that you can pick up. This focused attention not only helps you catch every word that your squad members say but also allows you to notice your squad members' moods and physical states. In addition, you'll get an idea of your squad members' feelings toward both you, and the other kids on the squad.

Listen Carefully

Perhaps more than anything else you do, how you receive messages from others demonstrates how much you care for the sender, and what he or she has to tell you. If you care little for your squad members or have little regard for what they have to say, it shows in how you listen to them. Check yourself. Do you find your mind wandering to what you're going to do after practice while one of your squad members is talking to you? Do you frequently have to ask a squad member, "What did you say?" If so, work on your receiving mechanics of listening. However, if you're always missing the messages that your squad members send, perhaps the most important question to ask yourself is, "Do I want to be a coach?"

Providing Feedback

We've discussed separately the sending and receiving of messages, but senders and receivers switch roles several times during an interaction. One person initiates communication by sending a message to another person, who then receives the message. The receiver then becomes the sender by responding to the person who sent the initial message. These verbal and nonverbal responses are called *feedback*.

Your squad members look to you for feedback all the time. They want to know how you think they're performing, what you think of their ideas, and whether their efforts please you. You can respond in many ways, and how you respond strongly affects your squad members. They react most favorably to positive feedback.

Praising squad members who have performed or behaved well is a good way to get them to repeat (or try to repeat) that behavior. Positive feedback for effort is an especially effective way to motivate youngsters to work on difficult skills. Rather than shouting and providing negative feedback to squad members who have made mistakes, try offering positive feedback in letting them know what part they did correctly and how they can improve. Oftentimes, just the way you word feedback can make it more positive than negative. For example, instead of saying, "Don't climb that way," say, "Climb this way." Then your squad members can focus on what to do instead of what not to do.

Positive feedback can be verbal or nonverbal. Telling young squad members, especially in front of the whole squad, that they have performed well is a great way to boost their confidence. A pat on the back or a high five communicates that you recognize a squad member's performance.

Communicating With Others

Coaching involves not only sending and receiving messages and providing proper feedback to your squad members, but also interacting with members of the staff, parents, fans, and coaches on the opposing side. Use the following suggestions for communicating with these groups.

Coaching Staff

Before you hold your first practice, it is important for the coaching staff to meet and discuss the roles and responsibilities that each coach will undertake during the year. Depending on the number of assistant coaches, the staff responsibilities can be divided into different areas. For example, one coach may be in charge of working with partner stunts, while another is responsible for teaching dance. The head coach has the final responsibility for all phases of the activity, but as much as possible, the assistant coaches should be responsible for their own areas.

Before practices start, the coaching staff must also discuss and agree on the following: terminology, plans for practices, game and competition organization, the method of communicating during practices, games, and competitions, and game and competition conditions. The coaches on your staff must present a united front and speak with one voice, and they must all take a similar approach to coaching, interacting with the

Coaching Tip
Although it is important for all of the coaches to share similar coaching philosophies and be able to work together, you and your assistant coaches don't have to be identical. On the contrary, look for assistant coaches who can complement areas where you aren't as strong. For example, perhaps you're confident in your ability to teach the fundamentals of leading a crowd, but you sometimes struggle with handling all of the logistics of reserving practice times or notifying parents and squad members of last-minute schedule changes. In this situation, consider recruiting an assistant coach or a parent to help you manage the duties of communicating game and practice schedules to the squad members.

squad members, parents, and one another. Disagreements should be discussed away from the sidelines or floor, where each coach can have a say and the staff can come to an agreement.

Preseason Meeting Topics

1. Share your coaching philosophy.

2. Outline necessary paperwork:
    *   Copy of birth certificate for the squad member
    *   Completed application and payment record for the squad member
    *   Report card from previous year
    *   Participation agreement form
    *   Informed consent form
    *   Emergency information card

3. Go over the inherent risks of cheerleading and other safety issues, and review your emergency action plan.

4. Inform parents of procedures involving uniforms and equipment, including what items the organization or squad provides and what equipment squad members themselves furnish.

5. Review the season practice schedule, including date, location, and time of each practice.

6. Go over proper gear and attire to be worn at each practice session.

7. Discuss nutrition, hydration, and rest for squad members.

8. Explain goals for the squad.

9. Cover methods of communication, such as an e-mail list, emergency phone numbers, or an interactive Web site.

10. Discuss ways that parents can help with the squad.

11. Discuss standards of conduct for coaches, squad members, and parents.

12. Provide time for questions and answers.

13. Have parents sign a statement indicating that they have discussed and understand the topics listed above.

Parents

A squad member's parents need to be assured that their daughter is under the direction of a coach who is both knowledgeable about cheerleading and concerned about their child's well-being. Put their worries to rest by holding a preseason parent orientation meeting, where you describe your background and approach to coaching. (See "Preseason Meeting Topics" for what information to cover at a parent orientation meeting.)

If parents contact you with a concern during the season, listen closely and offer positive responses. Messages sent to parents through squad members are often lost, misinterpreted, or forgotten. Always communicate important information directly with the parents.

Fans

Sometimes, fans may comment on your coaching actions or abilities. Acknowledging critical, unwarranted comments from a fan during a contest only encourages others to voice their opinions. Put away your "rabbit ears" and communicate to fans—through your actions—that you are a confident, competent coach.

Also, prepare your squad members for possible criticism from fans. Tell them to listen to you, not the spectators. If one of your squad members is rattled by a fan's comment, reassure her that your evaluation is more objective and favorable—and the one that counts.

3

Understanding Rules and Equipment

U nlike any other athletic activity, the primary focus of the cheerleading squad is to facilitate crowd support for the team on the field or the court. Oftentimes, coaches overemphasize the athletic aspects of cheerleading, such as stunts or tumbling. As a result, these aspects become the focus of the cheerleading squad, and subsequently leading the crowd then takes a back seat, and the true focus of cheerleading is lost.

This book is designed for coaches working with traditional cheerleading programs. In a traditional cheerleading program, the key functions of the squad are supporting the team, leading the crowd, and upholding, reflecting, and projecting the goals of the school and community. Although the sport of competitive cheerleading shares the same name, the purpose behind this activity is very different. This book focuses on traditional cheerleading. For information on competitive cheerleading, visit the US All-Star Federation at www.usasf.net.

Rules

There are no hard-and-fast rules for youth cheerleading, but there are safety guidelines that all cheerleading squads are encouraged to follow.

Safety

Coaches of all levels are encouraged to follow specific guidelines provided by the American Association of Cheerleading Coaches and Administrators (AACCA). The AACCA was founded in 1986 for the express purpose of providing safety education for cheerleading coaches and administrators. The AACCA works with state and local associations to provide cheerleading safety education to its members and has trained more than 20,000 coaches in their responsibilities to their squad members and institutions. In addition, the NCAA requires all Division I college cheer coaches to be AACCA certified. For more information on AACCA, please visit www.aacca.org.

The AACCA safety guidelines specify that safety should always be the primary focus for you and your squad members. Here are some main guidelines:

- The coach or administrator should provide adequate and appropriate supervision (more information on this appears in chapter 4).
- Squad members should learn to spot the most basic partner stunts and pyramids before progressing to more advanced skills.
- Spotters should be aware that the prime consideration of spotting is the protection of the performing squad member's head and spinal column.
- Spotters should be positioned directly next to the person being spotted. It is easier and more natural to reach up and catch the performing squad member when the spotter is already in the appropriate position and doesn't have to move.

- Spotting should be practiced from lower heights first; consistent, effective spotting should be demonstrated before spotters move to progressively higher stunts.

- All hard-surface practice areas should be covered with adequate matting (a minimum thickness of 1.25 inches), particularly for tumbling activities and stunts that are more than two persons high.

- Floors, as well as outdoor performing surfaces, should be level, smooth, clean, and dry.

- The use of a trampoline, mini-tramp, double mini-tramp, or vaulting board is not recommended for cheerleading activities.

Entering Competitions

Competitions are another fun and exciting way for traditional cheerleading squads to represent their school, organization, or community. As long as the traditional cheerleading program keeps its primary focus on leading the crowd and supporting the team, competing can become a rewarding experience for a squad.

Make sure that you select a cheerleading competition that best suits your squad. The competition should include a crowd-leading component (i.e., cheer and sideline) that reinforces the philosophy you're teaching during the regular season. Also, enter your squad into the proper division, which can vary from competition to competition. Most importantly, make sure that the competition is administered by a reputable company with an emphasis on fun and participation (for a listing of competition dates and locations, visit www.varsity.com).

Tryouts

Depending on your school or organization and the age range for your squad, you may or may not hold formal tryouts to select your squad. For example, on the younger end, all girls who are interested in cheerleading might be welcome to join the squad, whereas older groups in the middle-school range may be required to try out. Procedures largely depend on the age of the group you are working with, the number of girls interested in cheerleading, and the policies of your school or organization.

Knowing that tryouts for youth can be emotional and stressful, we suggest the following guidelines to help you navigate the selection process:

- Develop a contract stating the participants' and parents' responsibilities, the costs incurred, and the rules to be followed for both the tryout process and the actual cheerleading season.

- If at all possible, meet with the parents of the candidates before the tryout. Explain the tryout procedures, what is expected of the squad members, and answer parents' questions.

- Invite a representative from your school or organization's administration to serve as an overseer of the tryout and review scores.
- Show the results of the tryouts to your supervisors and inform them of potential problems (e.g., a squad member not making it back on the squad).
- Keep the candidates' scores confidential (only you, your supervisors, and the judges should have access to the scores). However, an individual participant and her parent or guardian should be shown her scores, if requested.

In addition, it is suggested that you set a specific timeline for the tryout process, as shown in "Sample Timeline for Tryouts," so that all participants and parents are aware of the tryout procedures.

Sample Timeline for Tryouts

Two Months Before Tryouts

- Meet with supervisors to reserve facility.
- Notify eligible participants about details of upcoming tryouts. Advertise with signs, flyers, and ads in the local newspaper and/or radio stations.
- Finalize forms, including score sheets, team rules, medical release forms, and parental permission slips, etc.
- Determine tryout format (e.g., younger teams often use a group tryout format, while older participants often try out as individuals.)

One Month Before Tryouts

- Hold a meeting with participants and parents to give an overview of the cheerleading program and answer any questions regarding the upcoming tryouts.
- Hand out all forms (medical evaluation, permission slips, etc.)
- Contact and select judges.

Week of Tryouts

- Collect permission slips and medical forms.
- Teach and review material at the tryout clinics.
- Assign groups if using a group tryout format.
- Confirm tryout time, date, and location with judges. They need to arrive 30–45 minutes prior to the time the tryouts begin.

Day of Tryouts

- Set up chairs and tables for judges. Hand out score sheets, calculators, pencils, and paper.
- Hand out nametags or numbers for all participants.
- Have a properly supervised staging area for participants to warm up and practice.

Equipment

Cheerleading doesn't necessarily require equipment in the traditional sense. However, uniforms, appearance, and visual aids help your squad members put together a unified look on the field or court at games or competitions.

Uniform

Uniforms should reflect a modest and appropriate athletic look. The uniform top should cover the midriff completely, and skirts should be an appropriate length. Skirt length should depend on the squad member's height and body shape (for youth, this is generally about 11 inches), and athletic shoes are always required. Depending on the weather and time of year, squad members may wear matching warm-up outfits that complement the uniform. For example, the warm-ups may have the same striping as the uniform and may be interchangeable with the uniform.

Pom poms are now considered more than just a visual aid and have become part of the cheerleading uniform. The pom colors should match or coincide with the uniform colors. There are many pom sizes, but the most popular for youth are 6-inch or 8-inch poms. You can vary the way your squad uses their poms—for example, each squad member can have the same-color poms (e.g., two red poms), they can have two different-colored poms (e.g., one blue and one gold), or each pom can be a combination of colors (e.g., a mixture of red, blue, and white).

Hair and Makeup

At the youth level, makeup should not be required or encouraged for traditional cheerleading. For all games and competitions, hair should be worn back off the face. Squad members should not wear any clips, bows, or hair pieces that contain metal. They can use cloth or rubber hairpieces to reduce the risk of injury when partner stunting or building pyramids.

Jewelry

Jewelry is not allowed in youth cheerleading because of the risk of injury. This includes necklaces, bracelets, watches, rings, and all body piercing (including small stud earrings).

Visual Aids

Visual aids are a vital part of cheerleading and leading the crowd for games. Visual aids such as signs, flags, lettered boxes, megaphones, and poms enhance your squad's presentation and help squad members get the crowd involved by providing direction and instruction on what to do or say. All props should be made of lightweight material and should be easy to hold, especially if they are to be used by a top person in partner stunts or pyramids. Visual aids should not be carelessly thrown from a stunt. For more detailed information on using visual aids with your material, see chapter 6.

Providing for Squad Members' Safety

Afer a fantastic play on the field, suppose that one of your squad members does a great toe touch but lands incorrectly and falls to the ground. What do you do?

You never want to see your squad members get hurt. But the chance of injury remains a reality of athletic participation. In this chapter, we will describe your legal responsibilities as a coach and steps you can take to minimize the occurrence of injuries. We will also provide you with general first aid and emergency response procedures.

Game Plan for Safety

You can't prevent all injuries from happening, but you can take preventive measures that will increase the chances for injury-free participation. Here are some items to consider:

- Physical examinations
- Physical conditioning
- Facilities and equipment inspection
- Matchups and inherent risks
- Proper supervision and record keeping
- Environmental conditions

Physical Examinations

It is recommended that your squad members have a physical examination before participating in cheerleading. Parents or guardians should sign a participation agreement (discussed in more detail later in this chapter) and an informed consent form to allow their children to be treated in case of an emergency. For a sample form, please see "Informed Consent Form" in appendix A on page 128.

Physical Conditioning

Squad members should be in shape to participate in cheerleading. They should have adequate cardiorespiratory fitness and muscular fitness.

Cardiorespiratory fitness involves the body's ability to use oxygen and fuels efficiently to power muscle contractions. As squad members get in better shape, their bodies are more able to deliver oxygen efficiently to fuel muscles and carry off carbon dioxide and other wastes. At times, cheerleading may require strength, flexibility, and physical exertion. Youngsters who aren't as fit as their peers often overextend while trying to keep up, which can result in light-headedness, nausea, fatigue, and potential injury.

Remember that the goals of youth sport are to participate, learn, and have fun. Therefore, keep your squad members active, attentive, and involved with every phase of practice. Watch closely for signs of low cardiorespiratory fitness; don't let your squad members overdo it as they build their fitness.

Muscular fitness encompasses strength, muscular endurance, power, speed, and flexibility. This type of fitness is affected by physical maturity as well as strength training and other types of training. Your squad members likely exhibit a relatively wide range of muscular fitness. Those with greater muscular fitness are stronger at running, tumbling, and jumping—all necessary skills for cheerleading. They also sustain fewer muscular injuries, and those that do occur tend to be minor. In case of injury, recovery is faster among youngsters with higher levels of muscular fitness.

Coaching Tip
Younger squad members may not know when they need a break for water and a short rest, so work breaks into your practice schedules. In addition, have water available at all times during the practice session. Your squad members have varying hydration needs, so allow them to drink water whenever they need it.

Two other components of fitness and injury prevention are the warm-up and the cool-down. Although young bodies are generally very limber, they can become tight through inactivity. The warm-up addresses each muscle group and elevates the heart rate in preparation for strenuous activity. Squad members should warm up for 5 to 10 minutes, using a combination of light running, jumping, and stretching. As practice winds down, they can slow their heart rates with an easy jog or walk. Have squad members stretch for 5 minutes to help prevent tight muscles before the next practice, game, or competition.

Facilities and Equipment Inspection

Another way to prevent injuries is to regularly examine the areas in which your squad members practice, perform, and compete. Remove hazards, report conditions you cannot remedy, and request maintenance as necessary. If unsafe conditions exist, either make adaptations to prevent risk to your squad members' safety or stop the practice, game, or competition until safe conditions have been restored. You can also prevent injuries by checking the quality and fit of uniforms, practice attire, and any protective equipment used by your squad members.

Matchups and Inherent Risks

It is recommended that you group squad members in 2-year age increments. With narrow age ranges, you encounter fewer mismatches in physical maturation. Even so, two 12-year-old girls might differ by 60 pounds in weight, a foot in height, and 3 or 4 years in emotional and intellectual maturity, a difference that can present dangers for the less mature participants. Therefore, whenever possible, also attempt to match squad members so that they are of similar size and maturity. Such an approach gives smaller, less mature youngsters a better chance to succeed and avoid injury while providing more mature squad members with a greater challenge. Closely supervise practices, games, and competitions so that the more mature squad members do not put the less mature ones at undue risk.

You should also warn squad members of the inherent risks involved in participation in cheerleading. "Failure to warn" is one of the most successful arguments in lawsuits against coaches. Explain thoroughly the inherent risks of cheerleading and make sure that each squad member knows, understands, and appreciates those risks. Learn more about inherent risks by talking with the administrators of your organization.

The preseason parent orientation meeting is a good opportunity to explain the risks of the sport to both parents and squad members. It is also a good time to have them both sign a participation agreement form or waiver releasing you from liability should an injury occur. Work with your organization in creating these forms or waivers; legal counsel should review them before presentation. These forms or waivers do not relieve you of responsibility for your squad members' well-being, but they are recommended by lawyers and may help you in the event of a lawsuit.

Proper Supervision and Record Keeping

General supervision means that you are in the area of activity, and you can see and hear what is happening. You should be

- in position to supervise the squad before the formal practice begins,
- immediately accessible and able to oversee the entire activity,
- alert to conditions that may be dangerous to your squad members and ready to take action to protect them,
- able to react immediately and appropriately to emergencies, and
- present until the last squad member has been picked up after the practice or competition.

Coaching Tip

It's easier to provide specific supervision to a smaller group, regardless of age. Enlist the help of assistant coaches to divide your team into smaller groups in order to ensure that each squad member can practice skills in a safe environment. The more coaches present to help supervise, the better the squad members can learn and perform the skills of cheerleading. In addition, smaller groups allow each coach to provide more direct feedback to individual squad members.

Specific supervision is the direct supervision of an activity during practice. For example, provide specific supervision when you teach new skills and continue with it until your squad members understand the requirements of the activity, the risks involved, and their own ability to perform in light of these risks.

As part of your supervisory duty, you are expected to foresee potentially dangerous situations and be positioned to help prevent them. This requires that you know cheerleading well, especially the rules that are intended to provide for safety. Prohibit dangerous horseplay, and hold practices only under safe weather conditions. These specific supervisory activities, performed consistently, make the practice environment safer for your squad members.

For further protection, keep records of season plans, practice plans, and squad members' injuries. Request these forms from your sponsoring organization (see page 129 in appendix A for a sample injury report form).

Learning in Progressions for Safety

As a youth cheerleading coach, you need to be aware of the sense of infallibility experienced by young squad members. Most of them have never been seriously injured or had friends who were seriously injured, so they may not have a clear understanding of the risks involved in the athletic activity. They may be tempted to try more difficult skills before mastering the basics. When squad members learn partner stunts, pyramids, jumps, and tumbling in progressions, you have the responsibility to assess each squad member's progress, determine the proper ability level of that squad member, and decide when she can move on to more difficult stunts safely.

AACCA suggests that you document your squad members' progress using qualification forms (see sample forms on page 134 and 135 in appendix A) in order to provide written verification that you have used reasonable care to ensure their safety.

Environmental Conditions

Most health problems caused by environmental factors are related to excessive heat or cold, but you should also consider environmental factors, such as severe weather and air pollution. Making a conscious effort to ensure adequate protection for your squad members can prevent serious emergencies related to environmental conditions.

Heat

On hot, humid days, the body has difficulty cooling itself. Because the air is already saturated with water vapor (humidity), sweat doesn't evaporate as easily. Therefore, body sweat is a less effective cooling agent, and the body retains extra heat. Hot, humid environments put squad members at risk

Coaching Tip

Encourage squad members to drink plenty of water before, during, and after practice. Water makes up 45 to 65 percent of a youngster's body weight, and even a small amount of water loss can cause severe consequences in the body's systems. It doesn't have to be hot and humid for squad members to become dehydrated, nor is thirst an accurate indicator. By the time squad members are aware of their thirst, they may be long overdue for a drink of water.

of heat exhaustion and heatstroke (see more on these risks in "Serious Injuries" on pages 35–36). And if you are affected by the heat or humidity, these conditions are worse for the kids—not only because they're more active, but also because kids under the age of 12 have more difficulty regulating their body temperature than adults.

Cold

When a person is exposed to cold weather, body temperature starts to drop below normal. To counteract this reaction, the body shivers to create heat and reduces blood flow to the extremities to conserve heat in the core of the body. Regardless of how effective its natural heating mechanism is, the body withstands cold temperatures better if it is prepared to handle them. To reduce the risk of cold-related illnesses, keep squad members active to maintain body heat, and make sure that they wear appropriate protective clothing. Also monitor the windchill factor. Windchill can drastically affect the severity of squad members' responses to the weather. The windchill factor index is shown in figure 4.1.

Temperature (°F)

Wind speed (mph)	0	5	10	15	20	25	30	35	40
	Flesh may freeze within one minute								
40	-55	-45	-35	-30	-20	-15	-5	0	10
35	-50	-40	-35	-30	-20	-10	-5	5	10
30	-50	-40	-30	-25	-20	-10	0	5	10
25	-45	-35	-30	-20	-15	-5	0	10	15
20	-35	-30	-25	-15	-10	0	5	10	20
15	-30	-25	-20	-10	-5	0	10	15	25
10	-20	-15	-10	0	5	10	15	20	30
5	-5	0	5	10	15	20	25	30	35

Windchill temperature (°F)

Figure 4.1   Windchill factor index.

Severe Weather

Severe weather refers to a host of potential dangers, including lightning storms, tornadoes, hail, and heavy rains. Lightning is of particular concern at sporting events. For each 5-second count from the flash of lightning to the bang of thunder, lightning is 1 mile away. A count of 10 seconds means lightning is 2 miles away; a count of 15 seconds indicates that lightning is 3 miles away.

Cancel practice when your area is under a tornado warning, and take the appropriate steps to cancel or postpone competitions during such warnings as well. If you are practicing or competing when a tornado is nearby, go inside a building, if possible. If you cannot get into a building, lie in a ditch or other low-lying area, or crouch near a strong building. Use your arms to protect your head and neck, and instruct squad members to do the same.

The keys to handling severe weather are caution and prudence. Don't try to get that last 10 minutes of practice in if lightning is nearby. Don't continue to participate in heavy rain. Respect the weather and play it safe.

Air Pollution

Poor air quality and smog can present real dangers to your squad members. Both short-and long-term lung damage can result from breathing unsafe air. When the air-quality ratings are lower than moderate or when there is a smog alert, restrict the activities of your squad members. Your local health department or air-quality control board can inform you of the ratings for your area and when restriction of activities is recommended.

Responding to Injuries

Unfortunately, injuries can occur even when your squad members are careful. When injury strikes, you are likely to be the one in charge. The severity and nature of the injury determine how actively you are involved in the treatment. Regardless of how seriously a squad member is hurt, it is your responsibility to know what steps to take. Therefore, be prepared to take appropriate action and provide basic emergency care when an injury occurs.

Being Prepared

Being prepared to provide basic emergency care involves many things, including being trained in cardiopulmonary resuscitation (CPR) and first aid and having an emergency plan.

CPR and First Aid Training

If possible, it is recommended that all coaches receive CPR and first aid training from a nationally recognized organization such as the National Safety

Council, American Heart Association, American Red Cross, or American Sport Education Program (ASEP). CPR training should include pediatric and adult basic life support and obstructed airway procedures.

Emergency Plan

An emergency plan is an important part of being prepared to take appropriate action for serious injuries. The plan calls for three actions:

1. *Evaluate the injured squad member.*

   Use your CPR and first aid training to guide you. Be sure to keep your certifications up to date. Practice your skills frequently to keep them fresh and ready to use if and when you need them.

2. *Call 911 and/or the appropriate medical personnel.*

   If possible, delegate the responsibility of seeking medical help to another calm, responsible adult who attends the squad's practices and competitions. Write out a list of emergency phone numbers and keep it with you at practices, games, and competitions.

   Take emergency information for each squad member to every practice, game, and competition (see "Emergency Information Card" in appendix A on page 130). This information includes the person to contact in case of an emergency, what types of medications the squad member is using, what types of drugs the squad member is allergic to, and so on. Give an emergency response card (see "Emergency Response Card" in appendix A on page 131) to the contact person calling for emergency assistance. Having this information ready helps the contact person remain calm. Also, complete an injury report form (see "Injury Report Form" in appendix A on page 129) and keep it on file for every injury that occurs.

3. *Provide first aid.*

   If medical personnel are not on hand at the time of the injury, provide first aid care to the extent of your qualifications.

Emergency Steps

It is important that you have a clear, well-rehearsed emergency action plan. Be sure that you are prepared in case of an emergency. Your emergency plan should follow this sequence:

1. Check the squad member's level of consciousness.

2. Send a contact person to call the appropriate medical personnel and call or locate the squad member's parents.

3. Send someone to wait for the rescue team and direct them to the injured squad member.

4. Assess the injury.

5. Administer first aid.

6. Assist emergency medical personnel in preparing the squad member for transportation to a medical facility.

7. Appoint someone to go with the squad member if her parents are not available. This person should be responsible, calm, and familiar with the squad member. Assistant coaches or other parents are best for this job.

8. Complete an injury report form while the incident is fresh in your mind (see "Injury Report Form" on page 129 in appendix A).

Taking Appropriate Action

Proper CPR and first aid training, a well-stocked first aid kit, and an emergency plan help prepare you to take appropriate action when an injury occurs. Of course, you should provide first aid to the extent of your qualifications. But don't "play doctor" with injuries; sort out minor injuries that you can treat from those that need medical attention. Consider the appropriate action both for minor injuries and for more serious injuries.

Minor Injuries

Although no injury seems minor to the person experiencing it, most injuries are neither life threatening nor severe enough to restrict participation. When these injuries occur, you can take an active role in their initial treatment.

Scrapes and Cuts When one of your squad members has an open wound, put on a pair of disposable latex-free examination gloves or some other effective blood barrier and then follow these four steps:

1. Stop the bleeding by applying direct pressure with a clean dressing to the wound and elevating it. The squad member may be able to apply this pressure while you put on your gloves. Do not remove the dressing if it becomes soaked with blood. Instead, place an additional dressing on top of

Coaching Tip
Don't let fear of acquired immune deficiency syndrome (AIDS) and other communicable diseases stop you from helping an injured squad member. Check with your sport director, your organization, or the Centers for Disease Control and Prevention (CDC) for more information about protecting yourself and your squad members from AIDS.

the one already in place. If bleeding continues, elevate the injured area above the heart and maintain pressure.

2. Cleanse the wound thoroughly once the bleeding is controlled. A good rinsing with a forceful stream of water, and perhaps light scrubbing with soap, helps prevent infection.

3. Protect the wound with sterile gauze or a bandage strip. If the squad member continues to participate, apply protective padding over the injured area.

4. Remove and dispose of gloves carefully to keep yourself (and anyone else) from coming into contact with blood.

For a bloody nose that is not associated with serious facial injury, have the squad member sit and lean slightly forward. Then pinch the squad member's nostrils shut until the bleeding stops. If the bleeding continues for several minutes or if the squad member has a history of nosebleeds, then you should seek medical assistance.

Strains and Sprains The physical demands of cheerleading training, games, and competition can sometimes result in an injury to the muscles or tendons (strains) or to the ligaments (sprains). When your squad members suffer minor strains or sprains, immediately apply the PRICE method of injury care:

P Protect the squad member and her injured body part from further danger or trauma.

R Rest the area to avoid further damage and to foster healing.

I Ice the area to reduce swelling and pain.

C Compress the area by securing an ice bag in place with an elastic wrap.

E Elevate the injury above heart level to keep blood from pooling in the area.

Bumps and Bruises Inevitably, your squad members make physical contact with each other or with the ground. If the force applied to a body part at impact is great enough, a bump or bruise results. Many squad members can continue participation with such sore spots, but if the bump or bruise is large and painful, you should act appropriately. Again, use the PRICE method for injury care, and monitor the injury. If swelling, discoloration, and pain have lessened, the squad member may resume participation with protective padding; if not, arrange for the squad member to be examined by a physician.

Serious Injuries

Head, neck, and back injuries, fractures, or injuries that cause a squad member to lose consciousness are among the class of injuries that you cannot and should not try to treat yourself. In these cases, follow the emergency plan outlined on pages 32 and 33. However, your role in preventing heat cramps, heat exhaustion, and heatstroke is important. In addition, refer to figure 4.2 for an illustrative example of the signs and symptoms associated with heat exhaustion and heatstroke.

Heat Cramps   Tough practices, combined with heat stress and substantial fluid loss from sweating, can provoke muscle cramps, commonly known as heat cramps. Cramping is most common when the weather is hot. Depending on your location, it may be hot early in the season, which can be problematic because squad members may be less conditioned and less adapted to heat, or later in the season, when squad members are better conditioned but still not used to participating in cheerleading in high temperatures. A cramp, a severe tightening of the muscle, can drop squad members and prevent continued

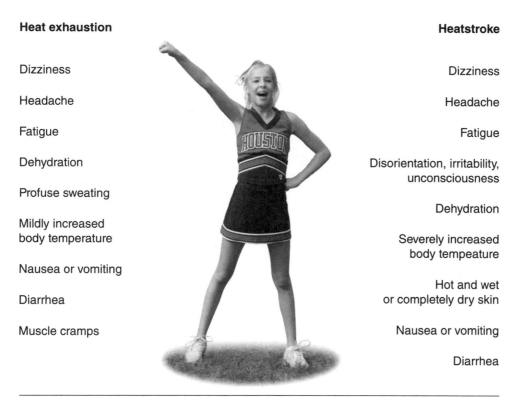

Heat exhaustion

Dizziness

Headache

Fatigue

Dehydration

Profuse sweating

Mildly increased
body temperature

Nausea or vomiting

Diarrhea

Muscle cramps

Heatstroke

Dizziness

Headache

Fatigue

Disorientation, irritability,
unconsciousness

Dehydration

Severely increased
body tempeature

Hot and wet
or completely dry skin

Nausea or vomiting

Diarrhea

Figure 4.2   Signs and symptoms of heat exhaustion and heatstroke.

participation. Dehydration, electrolyte loss, and fatigue are the contributing factors. The immediate treatment is to have the squad member cool off and slowly stretch the contracted muscle. A squad member may return to the sport later that same day or the next day, provided the cramp doesn't cause a muscle strain.

Heat Exhaustion　Heat exhaustion is a shocklike condition caused by strenuous activity combined with heat stress. This, in addition to dehydration and electrolyte depletion, results in symptoms that include dizziness, headache, fatigue, profuse sweating, nausea, vomiting, diarrhea, and muscle cramps. Difficulty with maintaining activity level and a mildly increased body temperature are key signs of heat exhaustion.

A squad member suffering from heat exhaustion should rest in a cool (shaded or air-conditioned) area with her legs propped above heart level; remove excess clothing and equipment; drink cool fluids, particularly those containing electrolytes (if not nauseated); and apply ice to the neck, back, or abdomen to help cool the body. If you believe that a squad member is suffering from heat exhaustion, seek medical attention. Under no conditions should the squad member return to activity that day, and it is recommended that she not be allowed to return to squad activities without a written release from her physician.

Heatstroke　Heatstroke is a life-threatening condition in which the body stops sweating and body temperature rises dangerously high as a result of strenuous activity in extreme temperatures. It occurs when dehydration and electrolyte depletion cause a malfunction in the body's temperature control center in the brain. Symptoms include dizziness, headache, fatigue, disorientation, irritability, nausea, vomiting, diarrhea, and the feeling of being extremely hot. Key signs include severely increased body temperature, skin that is either hot and wet or completely dry, rapid pulse, rapid breathing, seizures, unconsciousness, and respiratory or cardiac arrest.

If you suspect that a squad member is suffering from heatstroke, send for emergency medical assistance immediately, and cool the squad member as quickly as possible. Remove excess clothing and equipment, and cool the squad member's body by either applying cool, wet towels; pouring cool water over her; or by placing her in a cold bath. Apply ice packs to the armpits, neck, back, abdomen, and between the legs. If the squad member is conscious, give her cool fluids to drink. If the squad member is unconscious or falls unconscious, place her on her side to allow fluids and vomit to drain from her mouth. A squad member who has suffered heatstroke should not be permitted to return to the team without a written release from a physician.

Protecting Yourself

When one of your squad members is injured, naturally your first concern is her well-being. After all, your desire to help youngsters was what made you decide to coach. Unfortunately, you must also consider yourself: Can you be held liable for the injury?

From a legal standpoint, you must fulfill the nine duties that are discussed in this chapter (except for planning, which is discussed in chapters 5, 9, and 10). The following is a summary of your legal duties:

1. Provide a safe environment.
2. Plan the activity properly.
3. Provide adequate and proper equipment.
4. Match squad members appropriately.
5. Warn squad members of inherent risks in the sport.
6. Supervise the activity closely.
7. Evaluate squad members for injury or incapacitation.
8. Know emergency procedures, CPR, and first aid.
9. Keep adequate records.

In addition to fulfilling these nine legal duties, check your organization's insurance coverage and your own personal insurance coverage to make sure you are protected from liability.

5

Teaching and Shaping Skills

I n this chapter, we focus not only on teaching specific cheerleading skills, but also on teaching fitness concepts and values. Armed with these principles, you can design effective and efficient practices and understand how to deal with misbehavior. Then you can teach the skills (outlined in chapters 6–8) that are necessary for successful cheerleading.

Teaching Cheerleading Skills

Many people believe that the only qualification needed to teach a skill is to have performed it. Although it's helpful to have performed the skill, teaching it successfully requires much more than that. And even if you have never performed the skill before, you can still learn to teach successfully with the useful acronym IDEA:

I   Introduce the skill.

D   Demonstrate the skill.

E   Explain the skill.

A   Attend to those practicing the skill.

Introduce the Skill

Your squad members, especially those who are young and inexperienced, need to know what skill they are learning and why they are learning it. Therefore use the following three steps every time you introduce a skill to your squad members:

1. Get your squad members' attention.
2. Name the skill.
3. Explain the importance of the skill.

Get Your Squad Members' Attention

Because youngsters are easily distracted, do something to get their attention. You might use interesting news items, stories, or jokes. Or you could simply project enthusiasm to get your squad members to listen. Whatever method you use, speak slightly above your normal volume and look your squad members in the eye when you speak.

Also, position your squad members so that they can see and hear you. Then, before you begin to speak, ask whether all of them can see you.

Name the Skill

Although there may be many common names for the skill you are introducing, decide, as a staff, which name to use before the start of the season and then stick with it to help prevent confusion. When you introduce the new skill, call it by name several times so that the squad members automatically correlate the name with the skill in later discussions.

> **Coaching Tip**
>
> Writing out in detail each skill that you teach clarifies what you say and how you demonstrate and teach each skill to your squad members.

Explain the Importance of the Skill

As Rainer Martens, the founder of the American Sport Education Program (ASEP), has said, "The most difficult aspect of coaching is this: Coaches must learn to let children learn. Athletic skills should be taught so they have meaning to the child, not just meaning to the coach." Although the importance of a skill may be apparent to you, your squad members may be less able to see how the skill can help them become better at cheerleading. Give them a reason for learning the skill, and describe how the skill relates to more advanced skills.

Demonstrate the Skill

The demonstration step is the most important part of teaching a skill. Squad members need an image, not just words, so that they can see how the skill is performed. If you are unable to perform the skill correctly yourself, ask an assistant coach, one of your squad members, someone more skilled to perform the demonstration.

These tips help make your demonstrations more effective:

- Use correct form.
- Demonstrate the skill several times.
- Slow the action, if possible, during one or two performances so that squad members can see every movement involved in the skill.

Explain the Skill

Children learn more effectively when they're given a brief explanation of the skill along with the demonstration. Use simple terms and, if possible, relate the new skill to previously learned skills. Ask your squad members whether they understand your description and ask a squad member to repeat your explanation. Ask questions such as "What are you going to do first?" and "Then what?" If your squad member looks confused or uncertain, repeat your explanation and demonstration.

Complex skills are often better understood when explained in more manageable parts. For instance, if you want to teach your squad members how to do a thigh stand, you might take the following steps:

1. Show them a correct performance of the entire skill, and explain its function in cheerleading.

2. Break down the skill, and point out its component parts. First explain the responsibilities of the base person, then the top person, and finally the spotter.

3. Have squad members perform each of the component skills that you have already taught them, such as assuming the ready position and stepping and locking into the thigh stand.

4. Have squad members practice the skill in groups, with hands-on spotting, until the skill is mastered.

Coaching Tip

Technology improvements have created an opportunity to bring new demonstration methods to athletics. A variety of DVDs demonstrating various cheerleading skills are available. Consider using them as a tool to show skills, especially if you have difficulty demonstrating a particular skill or locating someone who can demonstrate it for you. This method can be especially effective with older squad members, who are better able to transfer the skills they see on the screen to their own performance.

Attend to Children Practicing the Skill

If the skill you selected was within the capabilities of your squad members and you have done an effective job of introducing, demonstrating, and explaining it, they should be ready to attempt the skill. Some children, especially those in younger age groups, may need to be physically guided through the movements during their first few attempts. Walking unsure children through the skill in this way helps them gain confidence to perform the skill on their own.

Your teaching duties, however, don't end when all of your squad members have demonstrated that they understand how to perform a skill. In fact, your teaching role is just beginning as you help your squad members improve their skills. A significant part of your teaching consists of closely observing the hit-and-miss trial performances of your squad members. You shape squad members' skills by detecting errors and then correcting them using positive feedback. Your positive feedback has a great influence on your squad members' motivation to practice and improve their performances.

Note that some children may need individual instruction, so set aside a time before, during, or after practice to give individual help.

Creating a Memory of Movement

Squad members need to develop a memory of movement—that is, learning a movement to a point where that movement occurs without conscious thought. An example might be performing a heel stretch on a side thigh stand. The top person finds that, by locking her leg, keeping her hips square, she can reach a balanced position with her hips over the base. Conversely, if she bends her leg, her hips move outside of the base and she falls to the side. After mastering this skill and remembering how her body feels and reacts in a certain position, she can duplicate the movement at other levels (e.g., from the shoulders in a large M pyramid or in a liberty).

Helping Children Improve Skills

After you have successfully taught your squad members the fundamentals of a skill, focus on helping them improve it. Children learn skills and improve on them at varying rates, so don't get frustrated if progress seems slow. Instead, help them improve by shaping their skills and detecting and correcting errors.

Shaping Children's Skills

One of your principal teaching duties is to reward positive effort and behavior—in terms of successful skill execution—when you see them. A squad member hits a new stunt in practice, and you immediately say, "That's the way to do it! Great job!" Your feedback, along with a smile and a thumbs-up gesture, goes a long way toward reinforcing that technique. However, sometimes you may have a long, dry spell before you see correct techniques to reinforce. It's difficult to reward children when they don't execute skills correctly. How can you shape their skills if this is the case?

Shaping skills takes practice on your squad members' part and patience on yours. Expect your squad members to make errors. Telling the squad member who hit her stunt that she did a good job doesn't necessarily ensure that she'll have the same success next time. Seeing inconsistency in your squad members' technique can be frustrating. It's even more challenging to stay positive when your squad members repeatedly perform a skill incorrectly or show a lack of enthusiasm for learning. It can certainly be frustrating to see squad members who seemingly don't heed your advice continue to make the same mistakes.

Frustration is normal when teaching skills, but part of successful coaching is controlling your frustration. Instead of getting upset, use these six guidelines for shaping skills:

1. *Think small initially.*

   Reward the first signs of behavior that approximate what you want. Then reward closer and closer approximations of the desired behavior. In short, use your reward power to shape the behavior you seek.

2. *Break skills into small steps.*

   For instance, in learning motions, one of your squad members has nice motion placement, but she is anticipating and hitting the motions too early. Reinforce the correct motion placement and teach her how to hit the motions on the proper word. Start with just one motion and then add others one at a time until she grasps the concept.

3. *Develop one component of a skill at a time.*

   Don't try to shape two components of a skill at once. For example, in partner stunting, each squad member has an important role to play, and each one must perform several skills in order for the stunt to hit properly. The base for a thigh stand focuses first on one aspect (proper lunge) and then on another (holding the top person's leg above her knee and pulling down into her body) and on yet another (spotting her waist for the dismount). Squad members who have problems mastering a skill are often trying to improve two or more components at once. Help them isolate a single component.

4. *Use reinforcement only occasionally—for the best examples.*

   By focusing only on the best examples, you help children continue to improve once they've mastered the basics. Using occasional reinforcement during practice allows squad members to have more time developing the many skills incorporated into cheerleading, instead of having to stop constantly and listen to your instructions. Cheerleading skills are best learned through a lot of repetition. Allowing the squad members as much time incorporating the skills into their cheers and sidelines as possible makes the best use of practice time.

5. *Watch and correct skill deterioration.*

   As a new skill is learned or as two or more skills are combined into one action, previously learned skills may deteriorate temporarily, and you may need to relax your expectations. For example, a top person has learned how to do a thigh stand and is now learning how to do a thigh stand with a heel stretch. While learning to pull up her outside leg into a heel stretch, the top person might bend her inside leg, which she hadn't done before.

6. *Go back to the basics.*

   If, however, a well-learned skill degenerates for long, you may need to restore it by going back to the basics. If necessary, practice the skill using an activity in which the squad members are under less pressure so that they can relearn the skill. For example, let a top person go back to the thigh stand without the heel stretch to ensure that she has mastered the step and lock of her inside leg.

Detecting and Correcting Errors

Good coaches recognize that children make two types of errors: learning errors and performance errors. Learning errors occur because children don't know how to perform a skill; that is, they have not yet developed the correct motor pattern in the brain to perform a particular skill. Performance errors are not made because children don't know how to execute the skill, but because they have made a mistake in executing what they do know. There is no easy way to know whether a child is making learning or performance errors, and part of the art of coaching is being able to sort out which type of error each mistake is.

Carefully watch your squad members to see if they routinely make the errors in practice, game, and competitive settings or if the errors tend to occur only during games and competitions. If the latter is the case, a squad member is most likely making performance errors. For performance errors, look for the reasons that your squad member is not performing as well as she can—perhaps she is nervous or maybe she is distracted by the game or competitive setting. If the mistakes are learning errors, help her learn the skill, which is the focus of this section.

When correcting learning errors, there is no substitute for your own mastery of the skill. The better you understand a skill—not only how to perform it correctly but also what causes learning errors—the more helpful you can be in correcting mistakes.

> **Coaching Tip**
> For older age groups or squads with advanced skill, ask squad members to "self-coach." With the proper guidance and supervision by the coach, young squad members can think about how they perform a skill and how they might be able to perform it better. Self-coaching is best done at practice, where a squad member can experiment with learning new skills.

Correct One Error at a Time

Suppose Megan, one of your tops, tends to bend her legs whenever she is extended in an elevator, which causes the stunt to come down. When she is being cradled she doesn't get her arms in proper cradling position. What do you do?

First, decide which error to correct first—young squad members learn more effectively when they attempt to correct one error at a time. Determine whether one error is causing the other; if so, have the squad member correct that error first, because it may eliminate the other error. In Megan's case, however, neither error is causing the other. In such cases, squad members should correct the error that is easiest to correct and that brings the greatest improvement and added safety when remedied.

Use Positive Feedback to Correct Errors

The positive approach to correcting errors includes emphasizing what to do instead of what not to do. Use praise, rewards, and encouragement to correct errors. Acknowledge correct performance as well as efforts to improve. By using positive feedback, you help your squad members feel good about themselves and you promote a strong desire to achieve.

When you're working with one child at a time, the positive approach to correcting errors includes four steps:

1. *Praise effort and correct performance.*

   Praise the squad member for trying to perform a skill correctly and for performing any parts of it correctly. Praise the child immediately after she performs the skill, if possible. Keep the praise simple: "Good try," "Way to stick it," "Good form," or "That's the way to lock out." You can also use nonverbal feedback, such as smiling, clapping your hands, or any facial or body expression that shows approval.

   Make sure you're sincere with your praise. Don't indicate that a squad member's effort was good when it wasn't. Usually a child knows when she has made a sincere effort to perform the skill correctly and she perceives undeserved praise for what it is—untruthful feedback to make her feel good. Likewise, don't indicate that a squad member's performance was correct when it wasn't.

2. *Give simple and precise feedback to correct errors.*

   Don't burden a squad member with a long or detailed explanation of how to correct an error. Give just enough feedback that she can correct one error at a time. Before giving feedback, recognize that some squad members readily accept it immediately after the error, but others respond better if you delay the correction slightly.

   For errors that are complicated to explain and difficult to correct, try the following:

   • Explain and demonstrate what the squad member should have done. Do not demonstrate what the squad member did wrong.

   • Explain the cause (or causes) of the error.

   • Explain why you are recommending the correction you have selected.

3. *Make sure the child understands your feedback.*

   If the squad member doesn't understand your feedback, she can't correct the error. Ask her to repeat the feedback and to explain and demonstrate how to use it. If the she can't do this, be patient and present your feedback again. Then have her repeat that feedback after you're finished.

4. *Provide an environment that motivates the child to improve.*

Your squad members won't always be able to correct their errors immediately, even if they do understand your feedback. Encourage them to "hang tough" and stick with it when they seem discouraged or when corrections are difficult. For more difficult corrections, remind them that improvement takes time and only happens if they work at it. Encourage squad members who have little self-confidence. Feedback like this—"You were hitting your heel stretch better today; with practice, you can improve your flexibility and extend that heel stretch even further"—can motivate a squad member to continue to refine her stunting skills.

Other squad members may be very self-motivated and need little help from you in this area; with these squad members, you can practically ignore step 4 when correcting an error. Although motivation comes from within, provide an environment of positive instruction and encouragement to help your squad members improve.

Team sports such as cheerleading provide unique challenges in correcting errors. How do you provide individual feedback in a group setting using a positive approach? Instead of yelling across the floor to correct an error during practice (embarrassing the squad member), have the squad take a short break. Then talk to the squad member off to the side of the practice area. You will find that the squad member is more receptive to the one-on-one feedback.

This doesn't mean you can't use the squad setting to give specific, positive feedback. You can do so to emphasize correct group and individual performances. However, use this squad feedback approach only for positive statements. Keep any negative feedback for individual discussions.

Dealing With Misbehavior

Young squad members misbehave at times; it's only natural. Following are two ways you can respond to misbehavior: extinction or discipline.

Extinction

Ignoring a misbehavior—neither rewarding nor disciplining it—is called extinction. This can be effective under certain circumstances. In some situations, disciplining young people's misbehavior only encourages them to act up further because of the recognition they get. Ignoring misbehavior teaches youngsters that it is not worth your attention.

Sometimes, however, you cannot wait for a behavior to fizzle out. When a squad member causes danger to herself or others or disrupts the activities of other members, take immediate action. Tell the offending squad member that the behavior must stop and that discipline will follow if it doesn't. If the squad member doesn't stop misbehaving after the warning, use discipline.

Extinction also doesn't work well when a misbehavior is self-rewarding. For example, you may be able to keep from grimacing if a youngster kicks you in the shin, but, even so, she still knows you were hurt. Therein lies the reward. In these circumstances, it is also necessary to discipline the squad member for the undesirable behavior.

Extinction works best in situations in which a squad member is seeking recognition through mischievous behaviors, clowning, or grandstanding. Usually, if you are patient, her failure to get your attention causes the behavior to disappear. However, be careful not to extinguish desirable behavior. When youngsters do something well, they expect to be positively reinforced. Not rewarding them likely causes them to discontinue the desired behavior.

Discipline

Some educators say that you should never discipline young people, but only reinforce their positive behaviors. They argue that discipline does not work, creates hostility, and sometimes develops avoidance behaviors that may be more unwholesome than the original problem behavior. Discipline doesn't always work and can create problems when used ineffectively, but, when used appropriately, discipline is effective in eliminating undesirable behaviors without creating other undesirable consequences. Use discipline effectively; it is not possible to guide your squad members through positive reinforcement and extinction alone. Discipline is part of the positive approach when these guidelines are followed:

- Discipline in a corrective way to help squad members improve now and in the future. Don't discipline to retaliate and make yourself feel better.

- Impose discipline in an impersonal way when squad members break squad rules or otherwise misbehave. Shouting at or scolding squad members indicates an attitude of revenge.

- Once a good rule has been agreed on, ensure that squad members who violate it experience the unpleasant consequences of their misbehavior. Don't wave discipline threateningly over their heads. Just do it, but warn a squad member once before disciplining her.

- Be consistent in administering discipline.

- Don't discipline using consequences that cause you guilt. If you can't think of an appropriate consequence right away, tell the squad member that you will talk with her after you think about it. Depending on age, you might consider involving the squad member in designing a consequence.

- Once the discipline is completed, don't make a squad member think that she is "in the doghouse." Always make her believe that she's a valued member of the squad.

- Make sure that what you think is discipline isn't perceived by the squad member as a positive reinforcement. For instance, keeping a squad member out of doing a certain activity or portion of the practice session may be just what she wanted.

- Never discipline your squad members for making errors.

- Never use physical activity—running laps or doing push-ups—as discipline. To do so only causes squad members to resent the physical activity that you want them to learn to enjoy throughout their lives.

- Discipline sparingly. Constant discipline and criticism causes squad members to turn their interests elsewhere and to resent you as well.

Coaching Tip

Involve older squad members in the process of setting squad rules and the consequences for breaking them. For example, they can brainstorm ideas for discipline in common situations, such as being late for practice, criticizing another squad member, or talking back to you. Once you've agreed on a list of rules and consequences, have each squad member sign the rules to cement her willingness to abide by them.

6

Cheers, Sidelines, and Dances

Whether you are coaching a cheer, sideline, or dance routine during a game, always remember the role of the cheerleading squad is to facilitate crowd support for the team on the field or court. Although this may sound simple, it is more complicated than you might think. There are many factors involved in engaging a crowd. For example, if your squad's team is on defense and the other team is about to score a touchdown, you don't want your squad doing a "We want a touchdown!" sideline. In that situation, a simple defense chant is most appropriate. Use material to get the spectators into the game and to entertain them. They have the most fun when they feel like they are a part of the game. Through effective use of cheers, sidelines, and dances, your cheerleading squad can help create that experience.

What are Cheers, Sidelines, and Dances?

A "cheer" has a definite beginning and end and should be used during an extended break in play (pregame, time-out, or halftime). Cheers are the best way for your squad members to incorporate stunts, jumps, and tumbling to lead the crowd. The general rule is that a squad should never do a cheer while the ball is in play. Here's an example of a cheer:

Two Bits!

Four Bits!

Six Bits!

A Dollar!

All for the Saints!

Stand Up and Holler!

A "sideline," however, repeats itself and should be the primary material used when the ball is in play. Even so, you can also use it during the extended breaks (pregame, time-outs, or halftime). Your squad members can set up and perform these sidelines in the same manner as the cheers. You can end a sideline by having the captain yell "last time" so that all of your squad members understand what to do. There is no hard and fast rule on when the stopping point is and your crowd is usually a good indicator of when to end the sideline. Here's an example of a sideline:

Gooooo, Tigers, Go!

[clap—clap—clap]

Gooooo, Tigers, Go!

[clap—clap—clap]

Gooooo, Tigers, Go!

[clap—clap—clap]

"Last Time"

Gooooo, Tigers, Go!

Dances

Dance routines are used to entertain the crowd during extended breaks, usually pregame or halftime (however, a short routine can be performed during a time-out if the game isn't too close). They are typically performed on the field or court.

Youth squads generally have only one dance per season, which they learn at a summer camp or at an organized dance class. However, you may be in a situation where you, the coach, are responsible for your squad's routine. If so, you can enlist the help of local dance instructors, teachers, coaches, or any other person with dance experience. Following are a few suggestions for creating a well-designed dance routine:

Choosing Style and Music

You have several options when choosing a style for your squad's dance. For example, you can select traditional styles, such as pom, kick, or jazz; or specialty styles, such as lyrical, modern, prop, or military. You can also combine several styles into one performance. On a related topic, as you are choosing a style of dance you will also need to select appropriate music. Here are some things to keep in mind when selecting music:

- Choose music that is easily recognized and enjoyed by your audience and that is appropriate for family viewing.
- Look for songs that have strong beginnings and endings. The first and last things the audience sees should be powerful and memorable.
- Don't use repetitive music. This may cause your audience to tune out. If you repeat choreography, that's perfectly acceptable, but it is not always necessary to repeat the music.

Choreographing the Dance

Developing choreography can be a trial-and-error experience—what works for one squad doesn't always work for another. Allow yourself leeway and don't be afraid to change your mind. Some things that show promise in your head and on paper don't always have the same effect on the performance floor. Whether this is your first time or hundredth time, always remember that creating choreography is a constant learning experience. The more you practice, the better you get!

As you are choreographing your squad's dance, know that an essential part of the dance is the blending of the different portions of the dance to make a solid routine. These transitions are a terrific way to change formations and move from one style to another smoothly. Transitions should happen quickly, free of unorganized movements and free of any collisions. Each element of your routine should be a pleasant surprise. Remember, too

(continued)

(continued)

few transitions can make your routine boring and too many can seem chaotic. Finding these new positions easily and showcasing the strengths of your performers will add visual highlights throughout your routine.

Teaching the Dance

To successfully teach a routine, here are a few things to keep in mind:

- Be sure the routine is finished before you begin teaching. Do not second-guess how quickly your squad will learn and prepare only a certain amount. Do, however, try to determine a good stopping point about a third of the way through the routine.
- Keep your routine notes nearby in case you need to refer to them.
- Practice teaching and using correct terminology before you actually teach.
- Count as if you are performing the routine with your voice—staccato for sharp motions and smooth for fluid movement.
- Use vocal cues and lead-ins. When rehearsing, give a four-count lead before the step. Use the same tempo you wish for them to continue in. Don't forget to note the music arrangement (verse or refrain) or any changes or effects in the music.
- Use as few words as possible. Too much instruction will confuse your squad members and leave them lacking focus.
- Be specific. The more specific you are, the less the squad members will need to ask questions. Always pretend that the squad members can't see you and only by your verbal description can they learn the choreography.
- Progress at the rate of the majority of your squad—not fast enough to lose those who learn at a slower pace and not so slow that the squad members who are fast learners are bored.

Engaging the Crowd

Crowds become engaged in the game given the right situation and proper motivation. To help your squad members learn how to engage the crowd, use "Five Steps to Crowd Success"—five key things that your squad members should be aware of when they are in front of a crowd: unity, material, direction and instruction, delivery, and timing.

1. *Unity*

   Your squad's main goal is to lead the crowd and to create group pride. Achieve this by employing group dynamics in cheers and sidelines and by providing something to make the crowd behave as a unified group. Examples of group dynamics can range from everyone wearing the school or team colors all the way to painted faces, shaker poms, or hats.

2. *Material*

   A crowd's vocabulary is limited and its attention span is short. Ultimately, the crowd is there to watch the game. The crowd should not have to think too hard about following along, so keep the words simple and familiar so that they are easy to remember. Examples can range from one word, such as "Tigers" or "Defense," to "Let's Go, Cats" or "Beat Those Bears."

   Coaching Tip

   As a coach, help your squad members understand what material is appropriate and when. This depends largely on factors such as possession of the ball, the score of the game, or the time of the game (i.e., pregame, time-out, or half-time). These factors go a long way in helping you or your squad captain decide what material is appropriate for the current situation.

3. *Direction and Instruction*

   Your squad members must tell the crowd what to do, so you need to teach them every chance you get. A common way to help the crowd become involved is to use visual aids, such as signs. When using signs, be sure to keep them simple and easy to see; introduce them at the beginning of the cheer or sideline so that the crowd knows what to yell. In addition, before each game, you can also pass out a handout with the words of your cheers and sidelines. However, do not try to teach the crowd too many cheers and sidelines during a season. The key is to "keep it simple" for the fans!

4. *Delivery*

   Your squad's delivery is the key to involving the crowd. The delivery should be enthusiastic, positive, and encouraging for the crowd.

5. *Timing*

   Your squad members need to know when it's appropriate to make the crowd yell, so be aware of the game situation. Timing is important. For example, your squad members shouldn't be yelling "Defense!" when the team has possession of the ball. The key to proper timing is to be aware at all times of what is happening in the game.

Coaching Your Material

In cheerleading, it is important to teach material to your squad members in a three-step progression, as follows:

1. Learn the words to the cheers and sidelines.
2. Teach the motions that correspond to the words.
3. Incorporate stunts, jumps, or tumbling into the cheers and sidelines.

Words

Words are the most important part of a cheer or sideline: It is your squad's goal to engage the crowd and encourage them to yell those words. When coaching a young squad, first ensure that your squad members know the words and understand the situation in which a specific cheer or sideline should be used before learning the motions or incorporating stunts or tumbling into the cheer or sideline.

> **Coaching Tip**
> Also teach your squad members that cheers and sidelines should be performed naturally, without overly expressive facial expressions, so that the crowd is yelling with the squad members, not wondering why their faces are unnaturally contorted.

First, the words to your cheers and sidelines should be simple and easy for the crowd to understand, as discussed in step 2 of "Five Steps to Crowd Success." Second, repetition is key in teaching your squad members. Just as with the fans, you don't want to have too many cheers and sidelines in your portfolio. It is better to have a smaller amount of material that your squad members can perform well than to have an abundance of material that they don't perform very well.

Also make sure that your squad members are placing emphasis on the right key words, such as your mascot name, team colors, or letters. Emphasizing key words lets the crowd know exactly what to yell back. In addition, make sure that your squad members pace the words to the cheers and sidelines (i.e., they aren't performing them too fast or too slow) and that they are projecting loudly and naturally (avoid deep, barking voices or high-pitched squeals).

Motions

Like the words in your material, motions are an important part of helping the crowd know when to yell. Your squad members' motions emphasize the key words for a cheer or sideline, which then helps the crowd know when to respond. At the youth level, there is no need to get too clever with motions; doing so can confuse the young squad members and put your crowd into spectator mode rather than participator mode.

When presenting motions to your squad members, first teach them to place the motions with the words. When first teaching a cheer or sideline, break it down into segments. Teach your squad members a few motions with the words and then review them before moving on to the next part. Try to frequently start back from the beginning when you review so that you build on what they already know. As the coach, you may need to give them feedback to help them clean up their motions as they are committing them to memory. Don't just teach them the motions—placement and synchronization are equally important.

Once your squad members have learned how the motions fall into place with the words of the cheer or sideline, they must learn that their motions should appear sharp and crisp and should hit on a key word (e.g., "Go," "Tigers," or "Fight!")—not before or after it. For example, you will have a variety of high V's and you want to make them all look the same and hit at the exact same time. To help straighten and sharpen up your squad members' motions in a specific cheer or sideline, first find a starting point (i.e., the position right before the first motion is hit), count to three out loud, and have them hit the next motion when you say "three" (e.g., "1—2—Hit"). They hold that motion until you have verified that they are all correct, and then you move on to the next motion in the cheer or sideline.

You may be tempted to place squad members' motions for them. However, an essential part of this activity is helping them to develop their muscle memory. By showing or telling them what to do rather than actually placing their motions for them, you encourage the development of this muscle memory more quickly.

Incorporations

Incorporating stunts, jumps, and tumbling into cheerleading activities can be a great way to get the crowd's attention and facilitate a crowd response. However, the crowd's focus should be on the words, not the skills, so only use stunts and tumbling to emphasize key words in cheers or sidelines; squad members should never be building or tumbling during those key words. A balance needs to be achieved with incorporations: Too much incorporation can lose the crowd and turn participators into spectators.

Once your squad members have learned the words and motions to a cheer or sideline, start working on incorporations. Stay within the squad members' ability level when incorporating stunts and tumbling. Use minimal stunts and tumbling if your squad members aren't ready for advanced moves. In addition, be sure that squad members master the incorporations in practice so they can still feel comfortable and confident leading the crowd. To help determine this, see the Partner Stunt Qualification Sheet and Tumbling Qualification Sheet in appendix A.

Basic Hand and Arm Positions for Motions

These motions make up the foundation for all of the moves squad members use in cheers and sidelines. Your squad members should hit these motions at precisely the same time during cheers and sidelines. They should focus on proper arm positioning, sharpness, and synchronization. The following are basic hand and arm positions for motions used in youth cheerleading:

Hand Positions

Buckets
Fists are positioned as if carrying a bucket.

Candlesticks
Fists are positioned as if carrying a candlestick.

Blades
Hands are held flat and fingers are completely extended.

Arm Positions

Daggers
Elbows are held into the side, with fists in line with the shoulders.

Punch
One arm is fully extended over- head and slightly in front, with the other arm on the hip.

Touchdown
Arms are extended straight overhead and slightly in front.

High V

Arms are in a V motion at approximately a 45-degree angle.

Low V

Arms are in an upside-down V motion at approximately a 45-degree angle.

Half High V

One arm is in a V motion at approximately a 45-degree angle, and the other arm is on the hip.

Half Low V

One arm is in an upside-down V motion at approximately a 45-degree angle, and the other arm is on the hip.

T Motion

Arms are fully extended out to the sides and slightly in front of the body.

Broken T

Elbows are out to the sides, with fists in line with the shoulders.

Half T

One arm is fully extended out to the side, and the other arm is on the hip.

L Motion

One arm is extended into a punch motion, and the other arm is in a half T.

Coaching Tip

Don't overdo incorporations and put too much into one cheer or sideline. The general rule of thumb is that cheers should have no more that two incorporations and sidelines should only have one. If you add too many stunts, it becomes distracting to the crowd and takes away from leading the crowd. The crowd's focus should be on the words, not on the skills.

Placement and Crowd Coverage

If possible, when performing cheers and side-lines, you and your squad members should set formations—the placement of your squad members on the sideline or on the field or court—that maximize the amount of space they have or are allowed to use. Ideally, you want them to position themselves in front of as much of the crowd as possible. When creating formations for cheers or setting game lines for the sidelines (see page 117 in chapter 9 for more information on game lines), keep in mind the height of each squad member. Set the formation so that taller members don't cover smaller members. It is also a good idea to place older squad members or those who may know the material better in the middle and front of the formations and game lines so that other squad members can follow their example.

Visual Aids

To maximize the effectiveness of a cheer or sideline, your squad members should make use of crowd-leading tools, called visual aids, as mentioned in chapter 3. These include signs, flags, lettered boxes, megaphones, and poms. Visual aids should give the crowd direction and provide instruction about what to do or say. Here are some tips when using visual aids:

- Introduce visual aids early. Your squad members should introduce visual aids at the beginning of your material so that the crowd knows what to do or say before the cue to respond. For example, when using signs, show them before the cheer or sideline so that the crowd is prepared to participate.

- Keep visual aids simple. Your squad members should not use long phrases on visual aids. For example, when using signs, stick to one word, letter, or symbol on each sign (e.g., one with the word "Go," another with the word "Fight," and one more with the word "Win").

- Consider the crowd's point of view. Your squad members should use visual aids—especially those with letters and words or those that require a crowd response—from left to right so that the people in the crowd can read and respond accurately from their point of view.

- Prompt the crowd for a response. Your squad members need to do something specific with the visual aid at the time that they are cueing the crowd for a response. For example, when using signs, they could implement a level change by raising the sign the crowd should be responding to above their heads, holding it up in a partner stunt, or moving it toward the crowd.

7

Partner Stunts and Pyramids

Partner stunts and pyramids are some of the most distinctive aspects of cheerleading. Over the years, their use has steadily increased the athleticism of traditional cheerleading. This chapter will provide you with a foundation to safely teach partner stunts and pyramids. We will outline the key technical points of stunts and pyramids by beginning with easier skills and then increasing in difficulty.

For both partner stunts and pyramids, you should monitor and document each squad member's progress using a Partner Stunt Qualification form (see page 134 in appendix A for a sample form). You can alter the sample form based on your needs and the stunts that your squad is performing. Most important, the form should list stunts in order, increasing in difficulty. Keep track of the dates that you approved stunts and review them individually with each squad member before she initials the form.

There are some initial rules to cover with your squad members. These rules should be followed at all times.

1. Use spotters at all times when learning or practicing partner stunts and pyramids until squad members have displayed proficiency.

2. Only use stunts that have been mastered as part of a pyramid.

3. When executing partner stunts and building pyramids, allow only one person—designated ahead of time—to speak. Typically, the speaker is you, the squad captain, or another designated squad member in a specific stunt group.

4. Designate a safety word, such as *down*, to use when a squad member doesn't feel comfortable with a specific stunt. She can say the word to cue others and to dismount the stunt safely.

5. Each squad member should clearly understand the methods involved in building and dismounting a partner stunt or pyramid.

Spotting for Partner Stunts and Pyramids

A spotter is a designated squad member in constant contact with the top squad members in a partner stunt or pyramid. The spotter should always be in a position to break the fall and catch the top squad member, with specific attention and care to her head and neck. By continuously touching the top squad member, it becomes instinctive for the spotter to catch or stabilize the top if she becomes unsteady. Spotting for partner stunts and pyramids requires the development of instincts that are essentially unnatural. For example, if a 100-pound object is falling toward you, your natural reaction is to move out of the way. Spotting, however, requires your squad members to move toward that object instead of away from it. Therefore, one of the most important ways to help keep your cheerleading program safe is to teach your squad members how to be good spotters.

To begin, there are essentially two types of spotting: hands-on spotting and general spotting. *Hands-on spotting* generally refers to spotting associated with learning new stunts and pyramids. Use this until squad members have mastered those stunts. With hands-on spotting, your squad members should do the following:

- Help the top get into proper position.

- Stand as close as possible to the top person as it is more natural to catch someone when you are already in position, rather than when moving toward a falling person.

- Be in constant contact with the top by continuously touching and holding her. If the spotter is unable to touch her, she should stand as close to the base as possible, with her hands up in the air.

- Keep their eyes on the top squad member at all times.

- Be in position to break the fall or catch the top, with the main focus on her head and neck, if she should become unsteady.

Coaching Tip

The first order of business for every squad should be to learn to spot effectively. A great way to start is to have your squad members dismount from the side of a set of bleachers to spotters standing on cushioned tumbling mats. An additional experienced adult spotter should always spot on the other side of the dismount until the entire squad becomes proficient. Start dismounting on the first bleacher and move up as the squad members perfect their spotting skills.

General spotting refers to spotting partner stunts and pyramids after the squad members have mastered them. The spotter should stand as close as possible to the squad member being spotted. She should be in position to catch her, no matter which direction she should fall in. Once a stunt group has displayed proficiency in the partner stunt and the spotting of the stunt using hands-on spotting, that group can progress to general spotting.

In addition to the two types of spotting previously described, the spotter is sometimes responsible for assisting the top squad member when she dismounts from a partner stunt or pyramid. This is called *catching*. There are two types of catches: the bear hug and the cradle.

For the bear hug, the spotter stands to the side and slightly in front of the top, who is dismounting with her arms up in the air (see figure 7.1*a*). As the top dismounts, the spotter's arms are above her head. She makes contact with the top by placing her outside arm and shoulder in front of the top and her head, other arm, and shoulder behind the top. The spotter's arms wrap around the top squad member as they would in a hug (see figure 7.1*b*). As the top descends, the spotter lifts upward, thus cushioning the impact of her dismount. The squad member who is dismounting must keep her arms up at all times to keep from hitting the spotter.

a   b

Figure 7.1   Bear hug dismount.

Coaching Tip

When teaching spotting to your squad, exercise caution when determining who is capable of spotting whom and work to instill three key aspects of spotting for partner stunts: first, stand close to the stunt; second, touch the top person in the stunt; and third, catch the top person as high in the air as possible.

The cradle catch is typically used for double-based or extended stunts. For the cradle, the spotter and the original base or bases are used. Most stunts at the youth level are double-based stunts, so the most common form of cradle is a three-base cradle using the two bases on each side and an additional squad member from behind to catch the top squad member's dismount.

When preparing for the dismount, the two bases become the catchers. They should be very close to each other and face each other with their arms up. A spotter in back should stand almost directly beneath the top squad member, with her arms up. The top should position her arms in a "T" and should look back behind her to make sure that the spotter is in place and is paying attention. The top falls back into the cradle in a rigid, open-pike position, with her shoulders and head up. She should keep her body tight and not lean back with her shoulders. The bases should catch the top by placing one arm behind her back and the other arm under her thighs. The spotter "blocks" the top's shoulders by placing her arms under each arm of the top squad member. The top should then wrap her arms around the bases' necks. See figure 7.2 *a-d* for an example of the cradle.

a

b

c

d

Figure 7.2   Cradle dismount.

Partner Stunts

Partner stunts are defined as one or more bases supporting one or more top persons off the ground (the functions of the bases and the tops are discussed in "Basic Partner Mechanics"). Partner stunts are performed during games to lead and entertain the crowd and are typically incorporated into a squad's cheers and sidelines. There are essentially three stages for partner stunts: climbing, climbing with weight transfer, and timing. When teaching partner stunts to your squad members, progress through the stunts in the order demonstrated here, moving on to the next stunt only when squad members have displayed proficiency in performing the skill.

Basic Partner Mechanics

As mentioned previously, for partner stunts, the top person—the *top*—is held off the ground by another squad member—a *base*. Both have specific responsibilities.

Base

The base supports the majority of the top squad member's weight while she is off the ground. When supporting a top, a base must control her hips by assuming the proper stance for the stunt being used and using her legs and hips to maintain balance in the stance. The base should also assist the top by resisting her climbing force as much as possible. For example, when the top in a shoulder stand pushes down, the base pushes upward to keep her arms straight.

Top

The top must be able to "climb lightly" by taking weight off the climbing foot and spreading its force and by keeping her body weight—called the center of balance—directly over the base in order to help ensure proper balance and stability (for more information, see "Climbing" in the "Basic Stunts" section). A top controls her hips by tightening her thighs and hips and straightening her legs by locking her knees. If the top squad member's lower body isn't tight, there is a greater tendency for her body weight to move outside the base, causing the group to lose balance.

Basic Stunts

The three stages of partner stunts are climbing, climbing with weight transfer, and timing. These are listed in progressive order, increasing in difficulty. Each stunt is given a number so that you can begin with the first stunt and work your way up as your squad members become proficient.

Climbing

The stunts included in the climbing group are basic stunts that help teach your squad members how to climb lightly. The stunts in the climbing group require adequate body strength, a keen sense of balance, and the ability of the participants to maintain the stability between themselves and the ground. Climbing skills help improve muscle memory for balance and control as well as enhance spotting and dismounting skills, as discussed previously in this chapter.

The following are common youth-level stunts that practice climbing skills:

Coaching Tip

To "climb lightly," the top squad member jumps off of her ground foot in order to take weight off her climbing foot. By jumping off the ground foot while simultaneously pushing down on the base's shoulders with her hands, the force or pressure of the actual step-up, or climb, is more evenly distributed, until her step-up leg is locked and the stunt is balanced.

1. STEP-UP

The base lunges with one leg bent so that her knee is over her foot and her other leg is straight, with her shoulders and hips facing front. The top places her hands on the base's shoulders and foot high on the base's thigh. A spotter then spots the top at the waist. See figure 7.3*a* for an example.

a   b

Figure 7.3   Step-up.

The top jumps hard off the ground and pushes through her arms, stepping up on the base's thigh. When standing, the top straightens and locks her climbing leg immediately by tightening her thigh and hip while keeping her hips facing the front. The top should make sure to lock her climbing leg and to use her hands to position most of her weight over the base's leg before she applies too much pressure on the base's leg. The base secures the top with her arm and hand by holding above the knee of the top's climbing leg and pulling down and into her own body. For a base who is lunging to the right, this is the right arm; for a base who is lunging to the left, this is the left arm. Her outside hand supports under the toe. A spotter spots the top at her waist. See figure 7.3b for an example.

To dismount the stunt, the top replaces her hands on the base's shoulders and lowers her leg back to the starting position on the ground. The spotter continues to spot the top at her waist as she steps down.

2. L-STAND

The base lunges with one leg bent so that her knee is over her foot and her other leg is straight, with her shoulders and hips facing front. The top places her hands on the base's shoulders and foot high on the base's thigh. A spotter then spots the top at her waist. See figure 7.4a for an example.

The top jumps hard off the ground and pushes through her arms, stepping up on the base's thigh. The top straightens and locks her climbing leg

a   b

Figure 7.4   L-stand.

immediately by tightening her thigh and hip while keeping her hips facing the front. Once the top has locked her climbing leg out on the base's thigh, the base secures the top with her arm and hand by holding above the knee of the top's climbing leg and pulling down and into her own body. For a base who is lunging to the right, this is the right arm; for a base who is lunging to the left, this is the left arm. For the L-stand, the top raises her inside leg at a 90-degree angle and the base supports it at her ankle. A spotter is positioned behind the top and spots the top at her waist. See figure 7.4b for an example.

To dismount the stunt, the base brings the top's leg forward to the front. The top then steps down to the front and the base grabs her waist. For the dismount, the spotter moves to the "step-up" leg side, continuing to spot at her waist as the top steps down.

3. SHOULDER STRADDLE

The base lunges with one leg bent so that her knee is over her foot and her other leg is straight, with her shoulders and hips facing front. The top places her hands on the base's shoulders and foot high on the base's thigh. A spotter then spots the top at her waist. See figure 7.5a for an example.

The top jumps hard off the ground and pushes through her arms, stepping up on the base's thigh. The top straightens and locks her climbing leg, tightening her thigh and hip while keeping her hips facing the front. When the top is standing on the base's thigh, she swings her inside leg to the front over the base's shoulder and sits, wrapping her legs under the base's arms and tucking her feet behind on the base's back, while the base holds on top of

a   b   c

Figure 7.5   Shoulder straddle.

the top's thighs and pulls down. At the same time the top is sitting, the base stands up so that her feet are positioned slightly wider than shoulder-width apart. A spotter is positioned behind the top and spots the top at her waist. See figure 7.5b for an example.

The top dismounts the shoulder straddle from the front. The base brings her hands outside of the top's legs and grasps her hands. The base dips with her legs, shrugs up quickly with her shoulders, and extends her arms, keeping them straight and locked throughout the dismount. The top pushes against the base's arms, assumes a pike position with her legs, and pops off the front. The spotter moves to the side and holds the top at her wrist with her inside hand and under her arm with her outside hand. See figure 7.5c for an example.

4. SIDE THIGH STAND WITH HEEL STRETCH

The base lunges with one leg bent so that her knee is over her foot and her other leg is straight, with her shoulders and hips facing front. The top places her hands on the base's shoulders and foot high on the base's thigh with her *inside* leg, rather than her outside leg as in the previous stunts. A spotter then spots the top at her waist. See figure 7.6a for an example.

The top jumps hard off the ground and pushes through her arms, stepping up on the base's thigh. The top straightens and locks her climbing leg, tightening her thigh and hip while keeping her hips facing the front. The top should make sure to lock her climbing leg and to use her hands to position most of her weight over the base's leg before she applies too much pressure on the base's leg. Once the top has locked out her climbing leg, the base secures that leg by holding her foot under the toe with her outside hand and the inner thigh with her inside hand. The base should make sure not to twist her shoulders as she holds the top; a twist increases the risk of the stunt collapsing. See figure 7.6b for an example.

For the heel stretch, the top assumes a stag position with her outside leg and uses her outside hand to grasp the middle of her foot as she pulls up into the heel stretch. The base keeps her hips facing front and supports the top's other leg at the ankle (if your squad members cannot perform the heel stretch, they can remain in the stag position with the outside leg). A spotter is positioned behind the top and spots the top at her waist. See figure 7.6c for an example.

To dismount the stunt, the top lowers her outer leg and steps down to the front as the base holds her at her waist. The spotter moves to the side and holds the top at her wrist with her inside hand and under her arm with the outside hand.

Climbing With Weight Transfer

The stunts included in the "climbing with weight transfer" group are basic stunts that help teach your squad members how to transfer their weight

a   b   c

Figure 7.6   Side thigh stand with heel stretch.

through their arms while continuing to step lightly, as described previously in the "Climbing" section that began on page 69. The stunts in this group also require adequate body strength, a keen sense of balance, and the ability of the participants to maintain the necessary stability between themselves and the ground. These skills help improve muscle memory for balance and control, as well as enhance spotting and dismounting skills, as discussed previously in this chapter.

Coaching Tip

To "climb lightly" while transferring her weight through her arms, the top should push down through her arms at the same time as the base locks her arms. This allows them to work together to distribute the weight off the feet.

5. SHOULDER STAND FROM A LUNGE

The base lunges with one leg bent so that her knee is over her foot and her other leg is straight, with her shoulders and hips facing front. The base extends her hands overhead and reaches back for the top's hands. The top grasps hands with the base and steps high on the base's thigh with her outside leg, or climbing leg. A spotter is positioned behind the top and spots the top at her waist as she climbs. See figure 7.7a for an example.

Holding the base's hands, the top jumps hard off the ground and steps up high on the base's thigh with her outside leg. For leverage, the top pushes

Figure 7.7   Shoulder stand from a lunge.

down through her arms as the base pushes up and locks her arms. See figure 7.7*b* for an example.

Still using the base's arms for leverage, the top places her inside foot on the base's shoulder, close to the neck, and locks the leg. The top then places her other foot on the base's other shoulder and locks that leg. As the top is stepping onto her shoulders, the base stands up, bringing her feet to shoulder-width apart. The base and top then release one hand at a time, and the base places her hands on the top's calves, pulling down as the top stands up. The spotter reaches up as high as she can, supporting the back of the top's legs, once the top is in the shoulder stand. See figure 7.7c for an example.

To dismount the stunt, the base releases her hands from the top's calves one at a time. The top grasps the base's hands without bending her legs, pushes through her arms, and steps off the front. The spotter moves to the side and holds the top at her wrist with her inside hand and under her arm with her outside hand. See figure 7.7d for an example.

6. DOUBLE-BASE SHOULDER STAND

One base lunges toward the other base with her leg bent so that her knee is over her foot and her other leg is straight, with her shoulders and hips facing front. The second base stands upright with her inside elbow close to her body and her forearm parallel with the ground. Both bases extend their outside arms overhead, and the top grasps the bases' hands. The top steps high on the first base's thigh with her outside leg, or climbing leg. A spotter is positioned behind the top and spots the top at her waist as she climbs. See figure 7.8a for an example.

The bases keep their arms locked and push up through their shoulders as the top pushes down through her arms and steps onto the lunging base's thigh with one foot and then to the standing base's arm with the other, locking each leg on each step. See figure 7.8b for an example.

With most of her weight shifted onto the standing base's arm, the top lifts her other foot so that the lunging base can grip the ball of her foot with her inside hand, with her thumb to the inside and her forefingers to the outside. The base then places the heel of the top's foot on her shoulder and stands up. The top steps up, locks her leg, and—putting most of her weight on her first base's shoulder—lifts her other leg so that the standing base can grip her foot with her inside hand under her foot, with her thumb to the inside and her forefingers to the outside. The standing base places it on her shoulder, just as the lunging base did, and the top locks her leg and distributes weight evenly on both shoulders. The top releases her hands from the bases' hands, one at a time, and stands up slowly so that she can maintain her balance. The spotter reaches up as high as she can, supporting the back of the top's legs, once the top is in the shoulder stand. See figure 7.8c for an example.

To dismount the stunt, the bases reach up with their outside arms, one at a time, and grab the top's hands. After the bases have grabbed hands again, the spotter moves to the side and holds the top at the wrist with her inside hand and under her arm with her outside hand. See figure 7.8d for an example. The top, without bending her legs, pushes through her arms and steps off the front. The bases keep their arms locked and catch the top under her arm, close to her body.

a   b

c   d

Figure 7.8   Double-base shoulder stand.

7. SHOULDER SPLITS

Before performing this stunt, the stunt group must determine the direction of the top person's split (i.e., which leg should be in front and which behind). In addition, the top should be sure to warm up adequately before performing this stunt.

Once the direction of the split is determined, the bases lunge toward each other. Both bases extend their outside arms overhead, and the top grasps the bases' hands. The top steps up onto the bases' thighs into a thigh stand.

a   b   c

Figure 7.9   Shoulder splits.

A spotter is positioned behind the top and spots the top at her waist as she climbs. See figure 7.9*a* for an example.

The bases dip, keeping their outside arms locked and connected with the top's hands, and the top dips with the bases, jumping into the splits while pushing down through her arms. If the top is splitting with her left leg forward, the base who is holding the top's left leg steps forward and places the leg onto her right shoulder. The base who is holding her right leg steps back and places that leg on her left shoulder. The top keeps her weight in her arms and lowers herself onto the bases' shoulders. The front leg base grips her ankle with her inside hand; the back leg base brings her inside arm between her leg and her body, flipping it over and gripping her ankle (the outside hands remain connected throughout the entire stunt). The spotter spots the top at her waist. See figure 7.9*b* for an example.

For the dismount, the bases dip on a designated count and, while keeping arms locked, push upward on the top's legs and immediately turn to the inside to support her upper arms when landing. At the same time, the top pushes through her arms, bringing her feet together for the landing. The spotter remains positioned behind the top and spots the top at her waist throughout the entire stunt. See figure 7.9*c* for an example.

8. PICKUP SHOULDER STAND WITH POST

The post (who will also be the spotter), in a semicrouched position behind the top, grasps the top's ankles. The base positions herself in front of the top in a forward lunge. The base grasps hands with the top. See figure 7.10*a* for an example.

The top gets a good jump off the ground for momentum, and the post dips with her legs and lifts the top up, using her legs first and then continuing up through her arms and shoulders. As the top moves up, the base, keeping her arms locked, steps back slightly as the top pushes through her arms while lifting with her hips. The top bends at the waist, keeping her legs straight and locked and using momentum to ride her hips up. The base keeps her arms in a locked position above her head, keeping them in close to her head. When the top is above shoulder level, the post places the top's feet on the base's shoulders. See figure 7.10*b* for an example.

The top releases hands with the base, one at a time, and stands up. The base then places her hands on the top's calves, pulling down as the top stands up. The post remains at the back with hands high on the top's legs until the top is standing and is balanced (she then moves to the side to spot and prepare for the dismount). See figure 7.10*c* for an example.

a   b   c

d   e

Figure 7.10   Pickup shoulder stand with post.

To dismount the stunt, the base releases her hands from the top's calves. The top grasps the base's hands without bending her legs, pushes through the arms, and steps off the front. As the top lands on the ground, the spotter holds the top at her wrist with her inside hand and under her arm with her outside hand. See figure 7.10*d* and 7.10*e* for an example.

Timing

The "timing" group includes basic stunts that help teach your squad members about timing between the top and the bases and the ability of the top to lift through her shoulders to take weight off the bases during the lifting phase of a stunt. These stunts require adequate body strength, a keen sense of balance, and the ability of the participants to maintain the necessary stability between themselves and the ground. Timing skills help improve muscle memory for balance and control, as well as enhance spotting and dismounting skills, as discussed previously in this chapter.

Coaching Tip

For proper timing, the bases should first practice timing without the top. Once the top is added, she should lift through her shoulders to stand from the loading position, and the bases should follow the top's momentum to lift her into the stunt.

9. ELEVATOR TO SHOULDERS

Two bases face each other in a semicrouched position, with their backs straight and hands cupped with palms facing upward. The top stands slightly behind and in between the bases and places her hands on the bases' shoulders. A spotter is positioned behind the top and spots the top at her waist. The top jumps into the bases' hands, keeping her feet close together. See figure 7.11*a* for an example.

When the top places her feet in the bases' hands, the bases need to grasp, with their thumbs to the outside and their forefingers on the inside of her foot, supporting the entire bottom of the top's feet. A spotter is positioned behind the top and spots the top at her waist as she climbs. See figure 7.11*b* for an example.

While supporting most of her body weight in her arms and hands, all three dip together by bending their legs and the top pushes with her arms. The top continues to push through her arms and lifts with her shoulders, standing with locked legs, as the bases shrug up with their shoulders and raise the top to shoulder level. The bases' hands open up so that the majority of her foot is in their palms, with the fingers of their front hand at her toe and the fingers of their back hand at her heel. The spotter reaches up as high as she can, supporting the back of the top's legs, once the top is at shoulder level. See figure 7.11*c* for an example.

To dismount the stunt, the bases reach up with their outside arms, one at a time, and grasp the top's hands. After the bases have grabbed hands again, the

Figure 7.11   Elevator to shoulders.

spotter moves to the side. The top, without bending her legs, pushes through her arms, and steps off the front. The bases keep their arms locked and catch the top under her arm, close to her body. The spotter holds the top at her wrist with her inside hand and under her arm with her outside hand. See figure 7.11*d* and 7.11*e* for an example.

10. ELEVATOR TO EXTENSION

Two bases and a top person begin this stunt in the elevator position. On a designated count, the two bases dip slightly, keeping their backs and shoulders erect. The bases then lift the top person by pushing through the arms and

a   b   c

Figure 7.12   Elevator to extension.

shoulders until both arms are fully extended and locked. The bases should look up at the top person in the extended position. The top person keeps her body tight, with her legs locked and hips tightened during the dip and she lifts up with her shoulders as the bases lift her to the extended position. The top person should keep her shoulders erect and look forward, not down. See figure 7.12a and 7.12b for an example.

To dismount the stunt, the bases cradle the top, as described previously on page 66. Note that if your squad members have not yet mastered the cradle, the bases bring the top down to shoulder level and reach up with their outside arms, one at a time, and grasp the top's hands. The top, without bending her legs, pushes through her arms and steps off the front. The bases keep their arms locked and catch the top under her arm, close to her body. See figure 7.12c for an example.

11. ELEVATOR EXTENSION

Two bases face each other in a semicrouched position, with their backs straight and hands cupped, as shown previously for the elevator to shoulders stunt in figure 7.11a on page 80. The top stands slightly behind and in between the bases and places her hands on the bases' shoulders. A spotter is positioned behind the top and spots the top at her waist.

The top jumps into the bases' hands, keeping her feet close together. While supporting most of her body weight in her arms and hands, all three dip together by bending their legs and the top pushes with her arms. When the top places her feet in the bases' hands, the bases need to grasp, with their thumbs

Figure 7.13   Elevator extension.

to the outside and their forefingers on the inside of her foot, supporting the entire bottom of the top's feet. A spotter is positioned behind the top and spots the top at her waist as she climbs. See figure 7.13*a* for an example.

The top continues to push through her arms and lift with her shoulders, standing with locked legs, as the bases shrug up with their shoulders and raise the top overhead, extending and locking their arms. At the same time, the top pulls her body upward, keeps her legs and hips tightened, and reaches upward with her arms, looking straight ahead. Once the top is in an overhead position, the bases' hands open up so that the majority of her foot is in their palms, with the fingers of their front hand at her toe and the fingers of their back hand at her heel. The spotter reaches up as high as she can, supporting the back of the top's legs. See figure 7.13*b* for an example of the stunt.

To dismount the stunt, the bases bring the top down to shoulder level and reach up with their outside arms, one at a time, and grasp the top's hands. After the bases have grabbed hands, the spotter moves to the side. The top, without bending her legs, pushes through her arms, and steps off the front. The bases keep their arms locked and catch the top under her arm, close to her body. The spotter holds the top at her wrist with her inside hand and under her arm with her outside hand. See figure 7.13*c* and 7.13*d* for an example.

12. WALK-IN ELEVATOR

Two bases face each other in a semicrouched position, with their backs upright and their hands cupped. The top stands slightly behind and in between the bases and places her hands on the bases' shoulders. While supporting most of her body weight in her arms and hands, the top steps into the hands of one base (the *main base*) with the leg that she is most comfortable using, called the *support leg* (determined ahead of time so that the bases know which foot the top will be using). The main base grasps the foot of her support leg, with her thumbs to the outside and her forefingers on the inside, supporting the entire bottom of the top's foot; the secondary base's front hand grasps the main base's wrists and her back hand under her foot. A spotter is positioned behind the top and begins in a crouched position, similar to that of the bases, so that she can grab the ankle of the top's support leg with one hand and support her seat with the other hand as the stunt begins. See figure 7.14*a* for an example.

All three dip together by bending their legs and the top pushes through her arms, lifts with her shoulders, and stands, locking her leg, as the bases shrug

a   b   c

Figure 7.14   Walk-in elevator.

up with their shoulders and raise the top overhead, extending and locking their arms. At the same time, the top pulls her body upward, with her feet close together and keeping her legs extended and her hips tightened, while shrugging upward with her arms and shoulders and looking straight ahead. Once the top is in an overhead position, the secondary base releases the main base's wrists and grasps the foot of her free leg. The top must let the secondary base grasp her free foot, rather than attempting to place it herself. As the stunt goes up, the spotter keeps one hand on the ankle of her support leg and uses the other hand and arm to lift the top's seat, helping keep her hips in line with the bases. At the top of the stunt, the spotter brings her hand out from under the top's seat and grasps the ankle of her free leg to help pull her legs together. See figure 7.14*b* and 7.14*c* for an example.

To dismount the stunt, the bases cradle the top, as described previously on page 66. Note that if your squad members have not yet mastered the cradle, the bases bring the top down to shoulder level and reach up with their outside arms, one at a time, and grasp the top's hands. After the bases have grabbed hands again, the spotter moves to the side and holds the top at her wrist with her inside hand and under her arm with her outside hand. The top, without bending her legs, pushes through her arms and steps off the front. The bases keep their arms locked and catch the top under her arm, close to her body.

Pyramids

Pyramids are a combination of individual partner stunts that are connected for one unified visual effect. Like partner stunts, pyramids are performed during games to lead and entertain the crowd and are typically incorporated into a squad's cheers and sidelines. Your squad should not perform pyramids that include partner stunts that have not been mastered in practice. Before teaching pyramids to your squad, be sure to take another look at the safety points discussed at the beginning of this chapter.

Basic Pyramid Mechanics

Pyramids are connected groups of partner stunts. To connect partner stunts and create a pyramid, your squad members must learn some basic mechanics in order to build properly.

For all pyramids, squad members should build partner stunts before connecting into the pyramid using grips (see the following paragraph about pyramid grips). To dismount, the tops should release their connection before dismounting the stunts. It may be necessary for the individual stunt groups to step apart prior to dismounting so that they do not interfere with another stunt or dismount.

When building pyramids, the individual groups of partner stunts are generally connected by the tops using specific pyramid grips: an *interlocking* grip—stunt groups are connected by the tops grasping each other's arms—or an *overlapping* grip—stunt groups are connected by the tops placing their arms over each other's arms without grasping, with their hands in blades.

Basic Pyramids

The most common pyramids to teach your youth squad members are described here and listed in progressive order, increasing in difficulty. To help you, each pyramid is given a number so that you can begin with the first pyramid and work your way up as your squad members become proficient. In addition, a diagram of each pyramid is included to show you each squad member's positioning and placement.

1. SMALL STAG

The small stag pyramid, as shown in figure 7.15, consists of two side thigh stands with stags to the inside and one person standing in the center and holding the tops' inside feet at shoulder level. For the dismount, the squad member in the center brings the tops' legs around to the front. The tops step off the front with the foot that the center brought to the front, and the bases catch the tops at the waist.

Figure 7.15   Small stag.

2. SMALL LONG BEACH

The small long beach pyramid, as shown in figure 7.16, consists of two side thigh stands with heel stretches to the inside and one person standing in the center and holding the tops' inside feet above the head so that they are extended out. For the dismount, the squad member in the center brings the tops' legs around to the front. The tops step off the front with the foot that the center brought to the front, and the bases catch the tops at the waist.

Figure 7.16   Small long beach.

3. SMALL M

The small stretch pyramid, as shown in figure 7.17, consists of two side thigh stands with heel stretches to the outside and one person standing in the center using an interlocking grip with the two tops' inside arms. For the dismount, the person in the center releases the tops' arms, the tops bring down the heel stretch leg, and then step off the front. The bases catch the tops at their waists.

Figure 7.17   Small M.

4. SMALL TREE

The small tree pyramid, as shown in figure 7.18*a*, consists of one shoulder stand in the center, two shoulder straddles on either side of the shoulder stand, two squad members standing on each side, and two more kneeling on each side on the end. For the dismount, the top in the center shoulder stand grasps hands with the base and steps off the front. The bases catch the tops at the waist. The top in the shoulder straddles grasps hands with the bases and pops off the front.

A variation of the small tree pyramid, as shown in figure 7.18*b*, consists of one shoulder stand in the center, two shoulder straddles positioned forward and on either side of the shoulder stand, three squad members standing slightly forward of the shoulder straddles and the shoulder stand (one is directly in front of the shoulder stand and the other two are out to the side), and four more kneeling in front.

5. BIG M

The big M pyramid, as shown in figure 7.19 on page 89, consists of two shoulder stands with the top squad members in a heel stretch to the outside and one shoulder straddle in the center with the top using an interlocking grip with the arms of the tops in the shoulder stands. The bases for the shoulder stands should place their outside hand under the tops' inside feet for additional support as the tops pull the heel stretch. For the dismount, the tops in all three stunt groups grasp hands with their bases and step off or pop off the front.

Figure 7.18 *(a)* Small tree and *(b)* small tree variation.

Figure 7.19   Big M.

6. LARGE TREE

The large tree pyramid, as shown in figure 7.20*a*, consists of one elevator extension in the center (with a spotter behind this stunt), two shoulder stands on either side of the elevator extension, and two shoulder straddles on either side of the shoulder stands. For the dismount, the top in the elevator extension can be cradled (see page 66 at the beginning of this chapter for information on spotting and dismounts) or she can grasp the bases' hands and step off the front once they lower her to shoulder level. The tops in the shoulder stands and the shoulder straddles grasp hands with the bases and step off or pop off the front.

A variation of the large tree pyramid, as shown in figure 7.20*b*, consists of one elevator extension in the center (with a spotter behind this stunt), two shoulder stands positioned forward and on either side of the extension, and three shoulder straddles in front.

Figure 7.20 *(a)* Large tree and *(b)* large tree variation.

7. CLEMSON PILE

The Clemson pile pyramid, as shown in figure 7.21, consists of three rows, with three shoulder straddles in the front row, two shoulder stands in the second row positioned in the windows of the shoulder straddles, and one elevator extension in the third row positioned behind the shoulder stands (with a spotter behind this stunt). The tops in the shoulder straddles put their arms on their hips; the tops in the shoulder stands bend at the waist and place their hands on the inside shoulder of the tops in the shoulder straddles. The top in the elevator extension places her arms on the lower backs of the tops in the shoulder stands.

For the dismount, all stunt groups disconnect. The top in the elevator extension can be cradled (see page 66 at the beginning of this chapter for information on spotting and dismounts) or she can grasp the bases' hands and step off the front once they lower her to shoulder level. The tops in the shoulder stands and the shoulder straddles grasp hands with the bases and step off or pop off the front.

Figure 7.21   Clemson pile.

8

Jumps and Tumbling

Jumps and tumbling are generally used when your squad's team performs a good play or scores points in a game. Like partner stunts and pyramids, jumps and tumbling have increased the athleticism in cheerleading. They also represent exciting dimensions to encourage enthusiasm and spirit from the crowd.

Safety for Jumps and Tumbling

Although jumps and tumbling are an exciting, athletic part of cheerleading, there are safety concerns related to both activities that should be discussed with your squad members and their parents.

As discussed at the beginning of chapter 7, a spotter is a designated squad member who is in constant contact with a performing squad member and is in a position to break a fall or catch her, with specific attention and care to her head and neck. Spotters should be used until squad members have mastered the skill.

In addition, there are specific guidelines that deal with landing—for both jumps and tumbling—after the skill is performed:

1. Teach your squad members to avoid landing on their heads, necks, or backs; landing in these areas can result in serious injury or death.

2. Encourage your squad members to practice good landing techniques until they become automatic. Teaching them how to lessen the force of landing should be an important part of your program.

3. Teach proper landing techniques at "ground level."

4. Use "sighting" or "visual cueing" when you teach proper landing technique.

5. Before they try landing techniques from any level above knee height, squad members should be able to demonstrate good technique in a variety of basic rolls.

6. Regardless of the skill attempted, performing squad members should never land with their arms or legs fully extended or locked.

7. Caution squad members not to give in to a full squat position when they are absorbing the force of landing. This position can result in injury.

Training for Jumps and Tumbling

Jumps and tumbling in cheerleading require specific physical demands from your squad members, and they need to train accordingly. Specific areas of training to focus on for improved jump and tumbling skills include conditioning exercises designed to improve general fitness; training exercises that increase muscle strength, especially in the legs; and flexibility exercises that help squad members become or stay limber. As discussed in chapter 4, any physical activity should be preceded by an adequate warm-up to increase body temperature and include stretching to allow for a wider range of motion.

The following are a few exercises to use with your squad members:

Calf Raises

Calf raises are used in cheerleading to increase calf muscle strength. The squad member should stand with the front half of her foot on a solid step or bench, with a partner holding her arms for balance. She then lowers her heel to the full stretch range of the muscle, followed by a full extension on the ball of her foot to flex her calf muscle. Have squad members repeat this exercise 5 to 10 times, followed by a short period of rest. This set of 5 to 10 repetitions can be repeated 3 times.

Vertical Jumps

Vertical jumps are an example of plyometrics, which are exercises in which the muscle is stretched (loaded) before it is contracted. They are a valuable tool for strengthening the thighs and many other muscles used for jumping. The squad member dips down and explodes into a high vertical jump. On landing, she immediately dips again and jumps up. This exercise can be repeated 5 to 10 times, followed by a short period of rest. This set of 5 to 10 repetitions can be repeated 3 times.

Seated Straddle Lifts

Seated straddle lifts isolate the hip flexors that raise the leg into the air and strengthen the hip flexors and lower abdomen muscles that apply to jumps or similar skills. The squad member sits on the floor with her legs in a straddle position and her hands on an imaginary line between her knees for support. Her back is upright, with a very slight forward lean onto her hands. Then she lifts each foot individually 1 or 2 inches off the ground for 1 to 5 seconds, depending on strength level. Once adequate strength has been achieved over the course of several weeks, additional time can be added. For a more advanced variation of this exercise, the squad member lifts both feet off the ground at the same time. Or she lifts them off the floor and allows them to drop to just above floor level and then back to the 1- to 2-inch height in repetition without touching the floor. This exercise can be repeated 5 to 10 times, followed by a short period of rest. This set of 5 to 10 repetitions can be repeated 3 times.

Sit-Ups

Sit-ups are used to increase abdomen strength, particularly the muscles that are used to "roll" the hips under the body during toe touches and pike jumps. For a sit-up, the squad member begins on the floor, on her back with her knees bent and with her arms behind her head. From this position, she lifts her torso into a position above her waist before returning to this starting position. This exercise can be repeated 5 to 10 times, followed by a short period of rest. This set of 5 to 10 repetitions can be repeated 3 times.

Jumps

Jumps are an energetic way to show excitement after a spectacular team play and to encourage support and enthusiasm from the crowd. When teaching jumps to your squad members, it is important to first teach the basic mechanics of jumps before teaching the various types of jumps.

Basic Jump Mechanics

Good jump technique can be divided into four distinct parts: approach, height, form, and landing.

Approach

A good approach shows the squad member creating momentum by swinging her arms. However, she should perform this swing in a powerful yet controlled manner. She should start in a high "V" and swing her arms in as she begins to dip her legs. Timing is important in order for her arm swing, to help with the lift in the jump. The squad member's arms should be at their lowest part of the swing when her legs are at the deepest part of their dip. This allows her arms and legs to lift quickly into the air at the same time. During the approach, she may rise up on her toes but should avoid leaving the ground, which creates an additional burden on her leg muscles.

Height

The squad member should attempt to jump as high as possible, to give her enough time to perform the jump as well as make a safe landing. She can do this by using a strong jump that is timed with the lift given by her arm swing. For increased height, she should stop, or "block," her arms in the "T" position, which transfers energy from her arm swing to her body.

Form

In proper jump technique, the squad member is in the air, with her shoulders directly over or slightly in front of her hips. Her arms should be straight across in a "T" motion, with her shoulders and chest up. Toes should be pointed.

All jumps can be divided into a top half and a bottom half. For proper technique training, have the squad member focus on these halves separately. The top part remains the same for most jumps. Therefore, you can train every squad member to perfect the top half of her jump. The bottom part of most jumps varies, and that's what creates the various types of jumps.

Landing

In proper technique for landing, the squad member first must have adequate height in the actual jump. She should then land with her feet together, with the initial weight starting in the balls of her feet and rolling backward toward her heel, before she redirects the momentum into an upward rebound. If she lands flatfooted or with a heavy, loud, or exaggerated "thud," she is most likely not absorbing the landing using the technique just described. This kind of landing increases the potential for injuries such as sprained ankles, shinsplints, and injured knees.

Coaching Tip

If your squad members have difficulty with the landing for a jump, suggest that they lower the height of their legs until they can perform a safe landing using proper technique. As your squad members increase their muscle strength and improve their technique for each of the four parts of the jump, they can then increase the height of their legs.

Basic Jumps

There are several basic jumps to teach your youth squad members. These jumps are listed in progressive order, increasing in difficulty. To help you, each jump has been given a number so that you can begin with the first and work your way up as your squad members become proficient. In addition, each jump includes photographs showing the essential parts of the jump.

1. TUCK

For the tuck, as shown in figure 8.1, the squad member starts with her arms in a high "V" position. Her arms swing in front of her body and stop sharply in a "V" motion. Once she is in the air, she brings her knees up to her chest, with her toes pointed. She should not move her chest down to meet her legs; instead, she should draw up her knees to the chest area.

Figure 8.1   Tuck.

2. SPREAD EAGLE

For the spread eagle, as shown in figure 8.2, the squad member starts with her arms in a high "V" position. Her arms swing in front of her body and around into another sharp high "V" position. Once she is in the air, she spreads her legs, with her toes pointed, so that her legs and arms create an "X."

Figure 8.2   Spread eagle.

3. HERKIE

For the herkie, as shown in figure 8.3, the squad member starts with her arms in a high "V" position. She lifts with her arms, brings one hand to the hip and the other arm is up and close to the head. She raises both legs off the floor at the same time. Then she extends one leg, the lead leg, out completely straight, with her toe pointed. Her knee and the top of her foot point toward the ceiling. She lifts her other leg into a hurdle position to the side and slightly behind her body.

Figure 8.3   Herkie.

4. TOE TOUCH

For the toe touch, as shown in figure 8.4, the squad member starts with her arms in a high "V" position. Her arms swing in front of her body to help create momentum into an upward position. She raises both of her legs off the floor at the same time. Her arms meet her feet (or are above her feet) and touch her toes while her body is in the air. (Note that a spotter should be used for this jump until it is perfected.)

Figure 8.4   Toe touch.

5. PIKE

For the pike, as shown in figure 8.5, the squad member starts by facing to the side, with her arms in a high "V" position. Her arms swing in front of her body to help create momentum into an upward position. She raises both of her legs off the floor at the same time; her legs stretch out straight, perpendicular to her body. Her arms are held out straight in front of her body. (Note that a spotter should be used for this jump until it is perfected.)

Figure 8.5   Pike.

Tumbling

Tumbling involves specific skills using height and inversion of the body for a visual effect. This section provides an overview of the basic gymnastic skills used in youth cheerleading. However, it is recommended that you enroll your squad members in a gymnastics course at a local gym or dance studio rather than attempt to teach these skills at your practices. The course instructors are trained to teach and spot these skills properly, and the proper equipment is provided to ensure the safety of your squad members. In addition, before attempting the gymnastic skills listed here, your squad members should have basic body awareness and proficiency in lead-up skills such as forward rolls, backward rolls, and handstands. These are all reasons why the instruction of these specialized skills should be in the hands of professionals.

Before a squad member performs tumbling skills at a game, she should master the skill in practice and you should approve it for use outside of practice. You should monitor and document each squad member's progress using a Tumbling Qualification form (see page 135 in appendix A for a sample form). You can alter the sample form based on your needs and the gymnastic skills that your squad members are performing, but, most important, the form should list the skills in order, increasing from easier to more difficult. Keep track of the dates of approval and review them individually with each squad member before she initials the form.

Prior to performing any gymnastic skill, review the following safety rules with your squad members:

Coaching Tip

The primary purpose of spotting in cheerleading centers upon protecting each squad member from injury during the learning and execution of a skill. For more complex tumbling skills, particularly those involving a somersault motion, spotting should be reserved for qualified coaches or persons who possess sufficient training and experience in advanced spotting techniques. It is recommended that squad members enroll in a gymnastics course to learn tumbling skills.

1. Make sure the tumbling area is big enough and free of obstructions. The tumbling surface should be smooth, level, clean, and dry. Use appropriate matting for practicing gymnastic skills.

2. Develop a "traffic flow" plan ahead of time to ensure safe participation for all squad members. Be aware all of the time of what's going on so that you can minimize the risk of squad members running into each another while tumbling.

3. Be sure that your squad members warm up properly before they start the tumbling activity. Of course, stop training whenever a squad member appears to be injured or begins to show signs of undue fatigue.

4. To be safe when tumbling, squad members need to wear proper attire. They should avoid tumbling in clothing that is either too restrictive or too loose. Jewelry is prohibited.

Basic Tumbling Skills

The most common basic tumbling skills for youth squads are the cartwheel and the round-off. It is suggested that you begin with the cartwheel and work your way up to the round-off as your squad members become proficient. In addition, each tumbling skill includes photographs depicting the essential parts of the skill. The execution of these skills requires proficiency in lead-up skills (forward rolls, backward rolls, and handstands). Again, it is recommended that your squad members enroll in a gymnastics class that offers professional instruction in these skills.

In this section, we have included photographs of commonly used tumbling skills. These skills should be learned from trained professionals and these photographs are meant only to demonstrate proper form.

1. CARTWHEEL

For the cartwheel, as shown in figure 8.6, the squad member faces sideways in a stretched position, with her arms overhead and against her ears. She lifts her lead leg and steps through a side lunge, reaching up and out laterally with both arms, lifting her lead leg overhead while pushing against the ground with her flexed leg. Her arms should be straight and placed in alignment with one another, approximately shoulder-width apart. Her eyes should stay focused on her hands throughout. She passes through a straddled handstand position, stepping down with her lead leg and then her trail leg, and finishes facing the same direction as at the start. The timing of the cartwheel should be 5 beats (i.e., foot-hand-hand-foot-foot).

a   b   c

d   e

Figure 8.6   Cartwheel.

2. ROUND-OFF

For the round-off, as shown in figure 8.7, the squad member stands facing forward in a stretched body position, with her arms overhead and against her ears. She lifts her lead leg, steps forward into a lunge position, and forcefully kicks her rear leg overhead while pushing against the ground with her flexed leg. As her hands go to the floor, she turns her shoulders a quarter turn in a 1-2 sequence (similar to the cartwheel). Her trail leg should meet her lead leg overhead. As her legs come together past the inverted position, she executes an additional quarter turn with her hips, pushing vigorously with her hands and through her shoulders, and quickly snaps her legs down to stand vertically. The landing position is in the opposite direction from the start.

a   b   c

d   e

Figure 8.7   Round-off.

Advanced Tumbling Skills

Beyond the cartwheel and the round-off, there are several more advanced tumbling skills that you may see at the youth level. These include a back handspring and a round-off back handspring. These skills, in particular, should be learned from trained professionals only and the photos included here are for demonstration purposes only.

Back Handspring

a

b

c

d

Figure 8.8   Back handspring.

Round-Off Back Handspring

a

b

c

d

e

f

g

h

Figure 8.9 Round-off back handspring.

9

Preparing for
the Season

We hope you've learned a lot from this book so far; your responsibilities as a coach, how to communicate well and provide for safety, and how to teach and develop skills. Now it is time to start preparing for the actual season—how well you conduct your practices and prepare your squad members for games greatly affects not only their enjoyment and success throughout the season, but also your own experience as a coach.

Learning Sport Basics

At the youth level, many of your squad members might not know a lot about the sport for which they are cheering. At the beginning of your season, help your squad members learn some basics about the sport for which they are cheering for and how their material and responsibilities work with the sport. For example, when cheering for football, here are some sample questions that you can review with your squad:

- What does being on defense mean?
- What does being on offense mean?
- What do you do for opening kickoff and during the game kickoffs?
- What is a first down?
- What is a touchdown and how many points is it worth?
- What is an extra point?
- What is a two-point conversion?
- What is a time-out?
- What is an interception?

Creating a Squad Constitution

At the beginning of each season, preferably at the preseason parent orientation meeting, provide your squad and their parents with a "squad constitution," which covers all of the rules and procedures, provides information about the goals of the program, and explains the expectations of each squad member. Your athletic association should review and approve this constitution prior to its use, and cheerleading candidates and their parents should discuss it prior to tryouts. In addition, all candidates must sign a form denoting that they have read the constitution and agree to its terms before trying out for the team. Following are some specific areas you might include:

Purpose
This section should explain that the primary purpose of the cheerleading squad is to support athletics for the association.

Tryouts
This section should cover clinic information, eligibility requirements, skills to be demonstrated, and the selection process.

Practices and Games
This section should review the average number and estimated time of practices so that working parents and students can plan around them. Provide a monthly calendar so that schedules can be made in advance. This section should also cover the number of excused or unexcused absences and the consequences of exceeding the allowance. It should state that all practices, games, and competitions are supervised by the coach, assistant, or designated school official. This section should note that squad members are not released to practice stunts, pyramids, or gymnastics without the direct supervision of the coach, assistant, or designated school official.

Safety Regulations
This section should state that the squad will follow accepted cheerleading safety guidelines and provide a copy of these guidelines.

Summer Camp
This section should note that the squad will be attending a summer training camp (if applicable) and that the dates and location of the camp will be determined immediately following tryouts, if they have not already been determined.

Expected Behaviors and Standards
This section notes that, if your school or association has a "Code of Conduct" for students, all squad members must abide by these rules.

Competition
This section states how much time will be devoted to competitions and that the purpose of competition is to provide a place to recognize the efforts of the squad members and their athleticism.

Discipline
This section explains your suspension and dismissal policy and what qualifies as a reason for suspension or dismissal from the squad.

Acceptance
This section states that the squad member and her parents (or legal guardian) have read and understand the policies previously described for participation on the squad and accept them as governing participation.

Creating Season and Practice Plans

Every season before the first practice with your squad, you should sit down as a staff and develop a season plan. A season plan is essentially a "snapshot" of your entire season so that you are able to accomplish all that you need to. As you begin, keep in mind the following seven tips to get the most out of your practices:

1. Stick to a practice time or day agreed on as a squad or a staff. Have prepared consequences for tardiness and missed practices to implement if this occurs.

2. Start and end each practice as a squad.

3. Keep the practice routine as consistent as possible.

4. Keep organized in your approach during practice sessions by moving quickly from one activity to another and from one stage of training to another.

5. Tell your squad members what each practice includes before the practice starts.

6. Allow squad members to take water breaks whenever possible and have water available at all times.

7. Focus on providing positive feedback.

Coaching Tip

You may find it helpful to write down on a calendar each game for which your squad will be cheering. Then go back through the calendar and list each practice. You can then work through each practice listed on your calendar to create your practice plans, outlining what you hope to accomplish in each practice.

You should find that implementing your season and practice plans with your squad is fairly simple. Most cheerleading squads begin practicing a month or two before their first game of the season. At this time, before games begin, gear your practices toward getting your squad game-ready. This means that your practices should focus on your squad's primary responsibility of leading the crowd—meaning that practice time should be spent learning the material. For example, if your squad practices twice a week for an hour and a half each day, your preseason practice plan might look like this:

Tuesday, October 23	
10 minutes	Make announcements, outline the practice overview, and lead the warm-up.
15 minutes	Review and practice defensive sidelines.
15 minutes	Review and practice offensive sidelines.
	[Water break]
30 minutes	Practice stunts, using progressions.
	[Water break]
15 minutes	Review and practice cheers used for time-outs.
5 minutes	Review the practice.

After the season begins and after your first few games, you'll learn what needs to be covered at practice and adjust your practices accordingly. For example, if your squad members have trouble with certain sidelines or a specific cheer, you can spend more time at practices focusing on them. A plan for a practice during the season might look like this:

Thursday, January 19	
15 minutes	Make announcements, discuss the execution of material at the previous game, outline the practice overview that focuses on problem areas, and lead the warm-up.
20 minutes	Review and practice the "Tigers Get Up and Yell" cheer; the focus is on motions and transition into stunts while reciting the words.
	[Water break]
30 minutes	Review and practice sidelines; the focus is on motions for "Rebound! Pull It Down!," "Push 'Em," and "1—2—3—4." Review motions for "We Are Bull—Dogs!" when lines use opposing motions and go over the procedure for changing game lines at the end of each quarter.
15 minutes	Review stunts used in floor cheers; review any jumps and tumbling that squad members have displayed proficiency at.
	[Water break]
10 minutes	Review the practice.

Planning for Games

During your preseason practices, after your squad members have learned their material, begin making specific plans for certain aspects of the game that involve special procedures. The following are a few of the most common aspects of the game that require planned procedures:

Run-On

Your squad members should have a procedure for when their team runs onto the field or court.

First, as a coach, you can decide the best way for your squad to participate in the team's run-on. At the youth level, many squads form two lines on each side of the entrance where the team enters and yell a specific chant. Squad members can also use poms or other props for a visual effect. Depending on the age level and ability of your squad, you may, for example, have your squad members line up across the field or court and perform back handsprings or other gymnastic skills as the team runs on. To execute something like this successfully, however, you need to know how much room on the field or court is clear and available for your use. In addition, take time during the preseason to practice this performance on the actual field or court so that your squad members know the procedures and you can ensure their safety.

Also, if your budget allows or you have some art or craft items available through your school or organization, your squad could create a sign for their team to run through.

Team Introduction

For games, generally an announcer or other person introduces the starting players for both the home and away teams. At home, a special introduction may be used to excite the crowd and get the players pumped up for the start of the game. Decide what your squad will do at this time, based on these procedures. Many squads have a specific cheer or sideline to perform on their side of the field or court that is timed with the announcement of each player.

Depending on ability, some squads build stunts that are timed with the announcement of each player and use signs or other props in the stunts. For example, when a player's name is announced, your squad might execute a shoulder stand or double-base shoulder stand; the top holds a sign that reads "Go!" Your squad could then chant "Go! Reid! Go!," with the top raising the sign on each "Go!"

National Anthem

Once the teams have been introduced, sometimes the national anthem is played before the game begins. Most squads form a long line on the field or court, on the endline, or even along the sideline directly in front of the crowd. However you choose to line up your squad members, most important is their behavior at this time. Your squad members should be standing still and be quiet, with their full attention on the song and looking at the flag. They should not be talking or laughing at this time. Remind your squad members about the meaning of this song and that, as squad members, they need to lead by example; someone is always watching them.

Start of the Game

At the start of each game, your squad members should perform the same sideline, chant, or set of motions to ready the crowd, get them involved, and build tradition. After several games or seasons, spectators learn to expect this specific sideline at the start of every game and are ready to yell with your squad members. For example, your squad can form their game lines and circle the right pom above their heads while saying the word "Go!" in a slowly increasing volume like this: "Goooooooooooooooooooooooo . . . [the ball is kicked] . . . Go Saints!" Depending on ability, they could do the same thing using stunts such as shoulder stands or elevators.

Time-Outs

There are guaranteed time-outs during games for all sports. As a coach, you and your squad members need to communicate with the opposing squad before the game to determine which squad will perform cheers during which time-out. Generally, the home squad takes the first time out and then squads alternate back and forth (see Game Courtesies for the Opposing Squad for more information on planning for courtesies to extend to opposing cheerleading squads during games). As part of your material for the season, your squad should have several cheers to perform during time-outs, and you should have enough material to cover each of the time-outs for your squad. However, in special circumstances such as overtime, you may end up running out of cheers.

If this occurs, you should have two or three sidelines reserved for use. For these sidelines, you can plan ways to involve the crowd, incorporate stunts, or use signs. For example, your squad members can spread out directly in front of the crowd in three shoulder straddles or shoulder stands and use signs for a simple chant of "Let's! Go! Cats!, Let's! Go! Cats!" This not only fills the time during the time-out, but it also keeps the crowd excited for those last few moments of the game.

Game Courtesies for the Opposing Squad

For games, plan for a few courtesies to extend to the opposing team's squad. Here are a few suggestions:

- Before home games, your squad can prepare a "hospitality" area for the opposing squad, where squad members can go to get ready before and after the game. Provide snacks and drinks for halftime and after the game. Many squads have a sign-up sheet so that each squad member can take a turn at bringing refreshments throughout the season. Arrange for a staff member or parent to supervise this room.
- If possible, take time before a game to meet with the opposing coach and squad. At this time, the squad members introduce themselves and, as the coach, you communicate with the opposing coach about taking the field or court for cheers during time-outs.

Scoring Traditions

Your school or organization may already have a tradition for how to celebrate scoring; if not, your squad can work to create one. Here are a few suggestions:

- Recite a specific chant after each score, such as "Way to Go, Trevor, Way to Go!"
- Perform a specific jump after each score. For example, after each score, a different squad member can step out and perform a jump.
- Perform push-ups together as a squad along the endline, after each score, for the total number of points that your team has on the scoreboard.
- Perform a back handspring or other gymnastic skill, depending on the ability of your squad.

Similarly, there are certain times during a game that your team needs support from your squad and from the crowd. For example, in basketball, a player may be driving the ball all of the way down the court or a player from the other team may be driving the ball down the court and one of your players is defending him or her. In situations such as these, your squad can use the momentum of the game to generate support for your team. At this time, your squad can perform short, quick sidelines and repeat them throughout the entire play so that it is easy for the crowd to pick them up and yell with the squad. An example might be "Defense! [clap—clap] Defense! [clap—clap]."

Injured Player

There may be times during a season when a player, either on your team or the opposing team, is injured during a game. Your squad should have a plan in place if this happens to show support for the player and to provide an example for the crowd by displaying good sporting behavior. Many squad members stop what they are doing and all kneel down on one knee with their hands on their hips. Once the player is up or is helped off the field, the squad members stand up and clap.

10

Coaching on Game Day

Cheering at games provides the opportunity for your squad members to show what they've learned in practice. Just as your squad members' focus shifts from practicing to performing at the actual game, your focus shifts from teaching skills to coaching your squad members how to perform those skills at games.

In previous chapters, you learned how to teach cheerleading skills to your squad. In this chapter, you learn how to coach your squad members as they execute those skills at games. Here are a few important coaching principles that guide you before, during, and after the game.

Before the Game

Often, you focus on how to coach your squad during the actual game, but your preparations should really begin well beforehand. Ideally, a day or two before a game, you should prepare your squad in several ways—in addition to the cheer and sideline material and partner stunt, pyramid, jump and tumbling techniques. Depending on the age group you are working with, you need to create a specific "game plan" for your squad; make decisions on specific cheer material and partner stunts to use; and discuss pregame particulars such as what to eat before the game, what to wear, and when to arrive at the game.

Planning Material

Some coaches burn the midnight oil as they plan material for game day. However, your game plan doesn't need to be complex—especially at the youth level. Your focus should be on your squad members' memory of the cheers and sidelines, ability to lead the crowd effectively, use of correct skills and techniques, building of confidence and self-esteem, and having fun! Emphasize the importance of teamwork, of every squad member fulfilling her role on the sideline, and of every squad member doing her best. As you become more familiar with your squad members' tendencies and abilities, you can help them focus on specific skills that help them perform better. For example, if your squad members tend to stand around and watch the action, emphasize the importance of performing more sidelines to get the crowd involved and excited.

When developing your game plan, make sure that your squad members understand what you expect of them during the game. Take time at the beginning or end of each practice to discuss these expectations. During the week before a game, inform them of the material you think will work and that you plan to use in the game (see "Game Formation Sheet" on page 133 of appendix A). Depending on the age level, experience, and knowledge of your squad members, you may want to let them help you determine the material to call in the game. It is your role to help youngsters grow through the sport experience. Allow squad members to provide input and involve them at the planning level. This gives them a feeling of ownership. Rather than just "carrying out orders" for you, they're executing the plan of attack that they've helped develop. Youngsters who have a say in how they approach a task often respond with more enthusiasm and motivation.

Setting Game Lines

Setting game lines—the order and rows that your squad members assume on the sideline—was previously discussed in chapter 6 on page 60, but it is worth taking some time to mention again here. Game lines are often a sensitive subject because most squad members want to be in the front row. You can handle game lines without creating problems or animosity among your squad members. First, use the number of squad members to determine the number of rows to stand in and then rotate the rows by quarter, period, or half. For example, if you have 18 squad members, place them in 3 rows of 6 and then rotate the rows as you choose. Another way of setting the game lines is by arranging the lines according to age or seniority, placing the older squad members, who may know the cheer material better, in the front row. This method also gives the younger members someone to look to when they're unsure about material. Nonetheless, it is important to explain to the squad members and their parents at the beginning of the season how you have set the game lines and why (this could be a topic at the preseason parent orientation meeting, as discussed in chapter 2 on page 17). Information provided up front leads to less confusion and fewer arguments down the road.

Discussing Pregame Details

Squad members need to know what to do before a game, such as what and when to eat on game day, what clothing to wear to the game, what equipment to bring, what time to arrive, and how to warm up. Discuss these particulars with them at the last practice before a game. Here are guidelines for discussing these issues.

Pregame Meal

In general, the goal of the pregame meal is to fuel the squad members for the upcoming event, to maximize carbohydrate stores (a ready source of fuel that is easily digested and absorbed), and to provide energy for the brain. Some

Coaching Tip

A preset plan or routine that is used before every game can help alleviate nerves and build confidence in your squad members, especially those who are younger. A pregame routine also helps squad members forget their outside concerns and get into the frame of mind to focus on cheering the game.

foods, such as carbohydrate and protein, digest more quickly than others. Squad members should consume these foods rather than those high in fat, which digests more slowly. Good carbohydrate foods include spaghetti, rice, and bran. Good protein foods include low-fat yogurt and skinless chicken. Squad members should eat foods they are familiar with and that they know they can digest easily.

In addition, pregame meals can be a great time for your squad members to bond, so possibly plan to hold meals at squad members' homes, alternating for each game.

Coaching Tip
Depending on the event and the time of day, it's important for your squad members to stay hydrated and fueled while cheering the game, not just before the game. Consider working with parents to rotate the responsibility for providing water or sports drinks, along with nutritious snacks such as fruit or crackers, for longer events. See chapter 4 for guidelines on how much fluid your squad members should drink before, during, and after each game.

Clothing and Equipment

Unless the squad members are traveling a long distance to cheer, they should arrive in their squad uniforms or squad warm-up outfits. As described in more detail in chapter 3, the squad uniform typically consists of matching tops (shells or sweaters), skirts, poms, and cheer shoes and socks. A squad warm-up outfit usually consists of a sweatshirt or jacket and a pair of pants, which are worn to all games. Your squad members may use other equipment, such as signs or megaphones, but typically you are responsible for bringing this equipment to each game. Be sure to discuss equipment expectations and fees at the preseason parent orientation meeting, as described in chapter 2.

Squad members can wear tape, braces, or protective wraps—to prevent injury or protect current injuries—as long as they are cleared by a doctor to participate. Ask their parents to ensure that the squad members are wearing the required items when they come to the game. Of course, you can't be responsible for the maintenance or fit of any such devices. In addition, always make sure to get an official letter from a doctor specifying that the squad member is clear to participate or indicating what preventive measures are needed for her to cheer or attend practice.

Arrival Time

Your squad members need to warm up adequately before a game, so instruct them to arrive 20 to 40 minutes before game time, depending on the age group. Designate where you want your squad to gather as they arrive so that you can quickly see who is there and who is not. If you have problems with squad members coming late to games, consider making a squad rule stating that squad members won't get to cheer for a certain amount of time (quarter, period, or half) unless they arrive a designated amount of time before the game and go through the complete squad warm-up.

Warm-Up

Your squad members need to prepare for a game both physically and mentally once they arrive. Physical preparation involves warming up. We suggest that squad members arrive 20 to 40 minutes before the game to warm up, depending on the age group; with younger squads, members can arrive closer to game time so that they stay focused and don't become too tired.

The warm-up should consist of stretches and a brief review of the cheers and sidelines, jumps, tumbling, partner stunts, and pyramids to use for the game. In addition, make sure that the warm-up (and all partner stunts, pyramids, jumps, or tumbling done in the warm-up) is performed on an approved surface, as recommended by the AACCA (see www.aacca.org for more information). Before the first game, walk through the steps for how the squad members enter the field or court and where they line up for the warm-up so that everyone knows what to expect.

> **Coaching Tip**
>
> Although the site coordinator and officials have formal responsibilities for facilities and equipment, you should know how to ensure that the game is safe for all squad members. Arrive at the game site 45 to 60 minutes before game time to check the facility and make sure that the surface your squad members are cheering on is safe and approved by the AACCA. This precautionary measure helps you, as a coach, keep your squad members safe and allows you to make adjustments to your material, based on the facility, if necessary, before your squad members show up for the warm-up.

In addition, before the game, refrain from delivering a long-winded pep talk. Just help your squad members mentally prepare for the game by reminding them of the skills they've been working on in recent practices and focusing their attention on their strengths and what they've been doing well. Also take time to remind squad members about teamwork: cheer hard, be safe, and have fun!

Unplanned Events

Part of being prepared to coach is to expect the unexpected. What do you do if squad members are late? What if you have an emergency and can't make the game or are late? What if the game is rained out or otherwise postponed? Being prepared to handle out-of-the-ordinary circumstances helps you out when unplanned events happen.

If squad members are late, you may need to establish a certain amount of time (quarter, period, or half) during which they will sit out. Although this may not be a major inconvenience, stress to your squad members that being on time is important. First, part of being a member of a squad is being committed to and responsible for the other members. When squad members are late, they break that commitment. Second, squad members need to go through a warm-up to prepare physically to cheer the game.

An emergency may cause you to be late or to miss a game. In these cases, notify your assistant coach, if you have one, or one of the veteran parents that you will be late or entirely unable to attend the event. If notified in advance, another volunteer or a parent of a squad member might be able to step in for the game.

Sometimes a game is postponed because of inclement weather or for other reasons such as unsafe field conditions or other unexpected issues. If the postponement takes place before game day, call every member of your squad to let them know that the plan has changed. If it happens while you're on site and preparing for the game, gather your squad members and explain why the game has been postponed. Before you leave the premises, make sure that all of your squad members have left the game with their parents—in short, you should be the last to leave. In addition, if members of your squad plan to carpool with parents of other squad members or to be picked up by someone other than their parents, the plans should be made in advance and documented in writing.

Communicating With Parents

You lay the groundwork for your communication with parents in the parent orientation meeting, through which parents learn the best ways to support the efforts of their children, and of the squad as a whole, on the field. Help parents judge success on how their kids are improving through their performances and the amount of fun they're having.

In the preseason orientation meeting, encourage parents to refrain from making disparaging remarks. Instead, have them support the squad by their comments and actions.

To help promote this support, when time permits and as parents gather before a game and before the squad has approached the field or court, let them know, in a general sense, the squad's focus during the past week and your goals for cheering the game. Parents are important, but your squad members must come first during this time, so focus on them during the pregame warm-up.

After a game, come together quickly as a squad to discuss—and informally assess with parents if they ask or if the opportunity arises—how the squad did, based on meeting performance goals and cheering to the best of their abilities.

For more information on communicating with parents, see page 16 in chapter 2.

During the Game

Throughout the game, keep everything in proper perspective and help your squad members to do the same. Observe how your squad members execute the words and motions to their sidelines and cheers and the skills for partner stunts and pyramids. Notice how well they are cheering together. These observations help you decide appropriate practice plans for the following week.

> **Coaching Tip**
>
> Always stay focused on the primary responsibility of a cheerleading squad: *To help facilitate crowd support for the team on the field.* Too easily, you can get caught up in "the art" of cheerleading and lose sight of the squad's real role so that the squad becomes ineffective at leading the crowd. Avoid promoting a "watch me cheer" attitude rather than a "cheer with us" attitude.

Cheering at games is the short-term goal of your program. The long-term goals are helping your squad members learn the words and motions, partner stunt and pyramid skills, and rules of teamwork; how to become fit; and how to be good sports on and off the field. Your young squad members are "winning" when they are becoming better human beings through their participation in cheerleading. Keep that in mind when you coach. You have the privilege of setting the tone for how your squad members approach cheering the game. As long as you keep all of these aspects in proper perspective, your young squad members will likely follow suit.

Let's take a more detailed look at your responsibilities during a game.

Correcting Errors

In chapter 5, you learned about learning errors and performance errors. Learning errors occur because squad members don't know how to perform a skill. Performance errors are not made because squad members don't know how to execute the skill, but because they make mistakes in carrying out what they do know.

Sometimes it's not easy to tell which type of error squad members are making. Knowing your squad members' capabilities helps you determine whether they know the skill and are making execution mistakes or if they don't know how to perform the skill.

If they are making performance errors during a game, however, you can help squad members correct them. Squad members who make performance errors often do so because they have a lapse in concentration or motivation or because they are demonstrating common human error. The crowd or the excitement of the game can sometimes adversely affect a young squad member's technique, so a word of encouragement about concentration may help.

If you correct a performance error during a game, do so in a quiet, controlled, and positive tone of voice between quarters, periods, halftime, or when the squad member is on the sideline with you.

Behavior of Coaches and Squad Members

Another aspect of coaching on game day is managing behavior—both yours and that of your squad members. It is your responsibility, as a coach, to control your emotions when aspects of cheering the game aren't going as you hoped.

Coach Conduct

You influence your squad members' behavior before, during, and after a game. If you're up, your squad members are more likely to be up. If you're anxious, they take notice and the anxiety can become contagious. If you're negative, they respond with worry. If you're positive, they cheer with more enjoyment. If you're constantly yelling instructions or commenting on mistakes and errors, they may find it difficult to concentrate.

The focus should be on having a positive attitude, working together, and having fun. If you overorganize and are constantly yelling, you are definitely not making cheering fun. So how should you conduct yourself? Here are a few pointers:

- Be calm, in control, and supportive of your squad members.
- Encourage squad members often, but instruct them sparingly while they're cheering. Squad members should focus on their performance during a game, not on instructions from the sideline.
- If you need to instruct a squad member, do so in an unobtrusive manner—when you're both on the sideline. Never yell at squad members for making a mistake. Instead, briefly demonstrate or remind them of the correct technique and encourage them. Tell them how to correct the problem while they're cheering.

Conduct of Squad Members

You're responsible for keeping your squad members under control. Set squad rules for good behavior. If squad members attempt to fight, argue, badger others, yell disparaging remarks, and the like, it is your responsibility to correct the misbehavior. Initially, it may mean immediately removing disruptive squad members from cheering the game, letting them calm down, and then speaking to them quietly, explaining that their behavior is not acceptable for your squad. If they want to cheer, they must not repeat the action. Younger squad members are still learning how to deal with their emotions. As a coach, strive to remain calm during times when young squad members are having trouble controlling these emotions.

In addition, you and your squad members should show respect for the opponents, visiting cheerleaders, and officials by giving your best efforts and being civil. Don't allow your squad members to "trash talk" or taunt opponents, other cheerleaders, or umpires. Such behavior is disrespectful to the spirit of competition. Immediately remove a squad member from cheering if she disobeys your squad rules in this area.

Welfare of Squad Members

As a coach, you quickly learn that all squad members are not the same and that some may base their self-worth on their performance and the response from the crowd or fans. This idea can be impacted by coaches, parents, peers, and society. Help squad members focus on realistic personal goals—goals that are reachable and measurable and that help them improve their performance while having fun as they cheer. On game day, remind squad members to cheer hard, do their best, and have fun. When coaching during games, remember that the most important outcome of cheerleading is building or enhancing squad members' self-worth. Strive to promote this idea through every coaching decision.

Keeping the Game Safe

Chapter 4 is devoted to the safety of your squad, but it's worth noting here that safety during games is just as important as it is in practice. Here are a few guidelines for games:

- Use spotters for all partner stunts, pyramids, jumps, and tumbling until the squad member becomes proficient.
- Your squad members should only perform partner stunts, pyramids, jumps, and tumbling that they have mastered in practice.
- All partner stunts and pyramids should be performed with adult supervision.
- Recognize your squad members' ability level and limit their activities accordingly. "Ability level" refers to the talents of the squad as a whole; individuals should not be pressed to perform activities that have not been safely perfected. As discussed at the beginning of chapters 7 and 8, monitor your squad members' ability according to accepted teaching progressions and track this on a qualification form (see pages 134 and 135 in appendix A for forms to help you monitor your squad members' progress).

You're working to protect your squad members whenever possible, so don't hesitate to address a safety issue when the need arises. You and your squad should remain up to date on all new safety guidelines and techniques. (For proper training, consider attending a Varsity Brands summer camp. See www.varsity.com for more information.)

After the Game

When the game is over, your squad's main focus should be on taking the field or court in order to congratulate the coaches and the players on the team they're cheering for. After a game, be prepared to speak with the squad members before they leave about problems that occurred while they were cheering the game, to hold a brief postgame meeting to ensure that your squad members are on an even keel, and to make sure they're aware of upcoming practices or events.

End-of-Game Procedure

As the game ends, squad members want to focus on the team they cheered for, whether the team won or lost. In the last few minutes or seconds of the game, squad members may want to perform a specific sideline or partner stunt reserved solely for the end of games. As the season progresses, this helps the crowd react at the end of the game. Once the game has ended, there are several options for how to support the team. For example, you may have an additional chant for your squad members to repeat as they take the field or court and move, as a squad, toward the team. Or your squad could make a tunnel for the team players to walk through as they leave the field or court. However your squad members choose to end a game, they should make sure to congratulate the team and to support it at all times—win or lose.

Reactions After a Game

After the game, you can be most influential in helping your squad members keep the outcome in perspective, whether the team won or lost the game. Make sure your squad members celebrate a victory in a way that doesn't show disrespect for the opponents. It's okay and appropriate to be happy and to celebrate a win, but don't allow your squad members to taunt the opponents or to boast about their own team's victory. If their team was defeated, your squad members naturally are disappointed. But, after a loss, it is the squad members' responsibility to help the team players keep their chins up and maintain a positive attitude as they walk off the field or court. Winning and losing are a part of life, not just a part of sport. If squad members can handle both equally well, they'll be successful in whatever they do.

Postgame Team Meeting

After the game, gather your team in a designated area for a short meeting. Beforehand, decide, as a staff, what to say and who will say it. Be sure that the staff speaks with one voice after the game.

If your squad members have performed well while cheering in the game, compliment them and congratulate them. Tell them specifically what they did well and what they improved on from the last performance. This feedback reinforces their desire to repeat good performances. Don't use this time to criticize individual squad members for poor performances in front of other squad members, and don't go over skill problems and adjustments at this time. Help squad members improve their skills in the next practice, not immediately after cheering the game.

Finally, make sure that your squad members have transportation home with their parents or that alternative plans are prearranged and documented in writing. Be the last one to leave the game site in order to ensure full supervision of your squad members.

Appendix A

Related Checklists and Forms

This appendix contains useful checklists and forms for your cheerleading program. All of the checklists and forms that are mentioned in the text can be found here. You may reproduce and use these checklists and forms as needed for your cheerleading program.

Informed Consent Form*

I hereby give my permission for _____ to participate in _____ during the_____athletic season beginning on _____. Further, I authorize the school, club, or organization to provide emergency treatment of any injury or illness my child may experience if qualified medical personnel consider treatment necessary and perform the treatment. This authorization is granted only if I cannot be reached after a reasonable effort has been made to do so.

Parent or guardian: _____

Address: _____

Phone: (   ) _____ Other phone: (   ) _____

Additional contact: _____

Relationship to athlete: _____ Phone: (   ) _____

Physician: _____ Phone: (   ) _____

Medical conditions (e.g., allergies, chronic illness): _____

_____

_____

_____

My child and I are aware that participating in _____ is a potentially hazardous activity. We assume all risks associated with participation in this sport, including but not limited to injury (minimal, serious, catastrophic, and/or death), the effects of the weather, traffic, and other reasonable-risk conditions associated with the sport. All such risks to my child are known and appreciated by me and my child.

We understand this informed consent form and agree to its conditions.

Athlete signature: _____ Date: _____

Parent or guardian signature: _____ Date: _____

*This release is being provided to cheerleading coaches and teams as an example only and should not be mistaken or construed as legal advice. Any coach, team, association, etc. should consult with its own counsel prior to relying on this release to limit its liability.

From ASEP, 2009, *Coaching youth cheerleading* (Champaign, IL: Human Kinetics).

Injury Report Form

Date of injury: _____ Time: _____ a.m. / p.m.

Location: _____

Injured athlete: _____

Age: _____   Date of birth: _____

Type of injury: _____

Anatomical area involved: _____

Cause of injury: _____

_____

_____

Extent of injury: _____

_____

_____

Person administering first aid: _____

First aid given: _____

_____

Other treatment given: _____

_____

Referral action: _____

_____

_____

_____

Signature of first-aid provider: _____

Date: _____

From ASEP, 2009, *Coaching youth cheerleading* (Champaign, IL: Human Kinetics).

Emergency Information Card

Athlete: _____ Date of birth: _____
Address: _____
Phone: ( ) _____

Emergency Contacts

Parent or guardian: _____
Address: _____
Phone: ( ) _____ Other phone: ( ) _____

Additional contact: _____
Relationship to athlete: _____
Address: _____
Phone: ( ) _____ Other phone: ( ) _____

Insurance Information

Insurance company: _____
Address: _____
Named insured: _____ Policy number: _____

Medical Information

Physician: _____
Address: _____
Phone: ( ) _____

Is your child allergic to any drugs?   *YES*   *NO*
   If yes, please list: _____

Does your child have other allergies (e.g., bee stings, dust)?   *YES*   *NO*
   If yes, please list: _____

Does your child have any of the following? *asthma   diabetes   epilepsy*
   If yes, please list any special needs:_____

Is your child currently taking medication?   *YES*   *NO*
   If yes, please list: _____

Does your child wear either of the following?   *glasses   contact lenses*

Are there any other concerns about your child's health?   *YES*   *NO*
   If yes, please list: _____

_____

Parent or guardian signature: _____

Date: _____

From ASEP, 2009, *Coaching youth cheerleading* (Champaign, IL: Human Kinetics).

Emergency Response Card

Be prepared to give the following information to an EMS dispatcher. (Note: Do not hang up first. Let the EMS dispatcher hang up first.)

Name: _____

Number dialing from: (   ) _____

Reason for call: _____

Number of people injured: _____

Condition of injured: _____

First aid being given: _____

_____

Current location: _____

Address: _____

City: _____

Directions (please note cross streets, landmarks, entrance access, etc.):

From ASEP, 2009, *Coaching youth cheerleading* (Champaign, IL: Human Kinetics).

Sample Tryout Score Sheet

Candidate Name or Number: _____ Judge: _____

Category	Points possible	Points received	Comments
Communication skills (*20 points total*)			
Projection	5		
Voice	5		
Enthusiasm	5		
Crowd appeal	5		
Motion technique (*20 points total*)			
Sharpness	10		
Arm levels	5		
Correct fists	5		
Dance technique (*20 points total*)			
Fluidity	10		
Rhythm	10		
Jump technique (*20 points total*)			
Form	10		
Height	5		
Flexibility	5		
Tumbling technique (*20 points total*)			
Form	10		
Height	5		
Difficulty	5		
Total points	**100**		

Additional comments: _____

_____

_____

From ASEP, 2009, *Coaching youth cheerleading* (Champaign, IL: Human Kinetics).

Game Formation Sheet

Game: _____

Date: _____

Squad members in attendance:

1. _____ 11. _____

2. _____ 12. _____

3. _____ 13. _____

4. _____ 14. _____

5. _____ 15. _____

6. _____ 16. _____

7. _____ 17. _____

8. _____ 18. _____

9. _____ 19. _____

10. _____ 20. _____

Cheer:_____

Cheer:_____

From ASEP, 2009, *Coaching youth cheerleading* (Champaign, IL: Human Kinetics).

Partner Stunt Qualification Form

Squad member name: _____

Age: _____ **Grade:** _____

Season: _____

Partner stunt	Date approved	Coach's initials	Squad member's initials
Step-up drill			
L-stand			
Shoulder straddle			
Side thigh stand with heel stretch			
Shoulder stand from a lunge			
Double-base shoulder stand			
Shoulder splits			
Pickup shoulder stand with post			
Elevator to shoulders			
Extension from elevator			
Walk-in elevator			
Ground-up liberty			

From ASEP, 2009, *Coaching youth cheerleading* (Champaign, IL: Human Kinetics).

Tumbling Qualification Form

Squad member name: _____

Age: _____   **Grade:** _____

Season: _____

Tumbling skill	Date approved	Coach's initials	Squad member's initials
Forward roll			
Backward roll			
Handstand			
Cartwheel			
Round-off			
Front walkover			
Back walkover			
Aerial cartwheel			
Front handspring			
Back handspring			
Round-off back handspring			
Back handspring series			
Back tuck			

From ASEP, 2009, *Coaching youth cheerleading* (Champaign, IL: Human Kinetics).

Appendix B

Cheerleading Terms

base—A person who supports the majority of a top person's weight while the top person is off the ground.

captain—A squad member who is chosen to be the leader of the squad.

chant—A short, simple yell, usually with movements, which is repeated several times. A chant is usually performed on the sidelines.

cheer—A longer yell that involves motions and sometimes stunts, pyramids, jumps, or tumbling. A cheer is usually performed on the field or court.

choreography—The set arrangement of steps and movements.

coach—A person who instructs or teaches squad members.

competition—An event in which squads come together to test their skills against other squads.

cradle—A dismount from a partner stunt, pyramid, or toss in which the top person is caught in a faceup, pike position before being placed on the performance area or remounting into another stunt, pyramid, or loading position.

execution—Performance of a stunt or routine; also, how a stunt or routine is performed.

extended stunt—When the entire body of the top person is extended in an upright position over the bases. Chairs, torches, flatbacks, and straddle lifts are examples of stunts in which the bases' arms are extended overhead, but these are *not* considered to be extended stunts because the height of the body of the top person is similar to that for a shoulder-level stunt.

loading position—A position in which the top person is off the ground in continuous movement that puts the bases and top in a position to end the movement in a stunt.

mascot—An animal, object, or person adopted by a squad as a symbol of the school or squad.

megaphone—A funnel-shaped device used to amplify and direct a coach's or squad member's voice.

motion—A set position of a squad member's arms and hands.

pom—A handheld ball of strips of plastic or other material connected by a handle.

routine—A continuous show of cheers, chants, and dance steps.

spotter—A person who is responsible for assisting or catching the top person in a partner stunt or pyramid. This person cannot be in a position of providing primary support for a top person, but she must be in a position to protect the top person coming off a stunt or pyramid.

squad—A small group of people organized for a specific purpose; an athletic team.

stunt—One or more bases supporting one or more top persons off the ground.

top—A person who is held off the floor by another person or persons.

Appendix C

42 Cheers and Sidelines

Whether you are a new coach who needs to create a foundation of material for your squad to use or an experienced coach who wants to add more material to what you already have developed, it's always a good idea to have a list of possibilities to choose from or to be inspired by. The following list includes several basic cheers and sidelines to use with your squad. These cheers and sidelines are designed to give you structures that you can then adapt to the specifics of your squad members and the team they are cheering for.

Cheers

You say Go, on the count of three
1—2—3—Go!
You say Cats, on the count of three
1—2—3—Cats!
1—2—3—Go!
1—2—3—Cats!

• • • • •

Tigers, get up and yell!
Go—Big—Red! [pause] Go—Big—Red!
Tigers, get up and yell!
Beat—Those—Bears! [pause] Beat—Those—Bears!
Go—Big—Red! [pause] Beat—Those—Bears!

• • • • •

Central fans on this side, yell, "Go!" [pause] Go!
Central fans in the middle, yell, "Fight!" [pause] Fight!
Central fans on the end, yell, "Win!" [pause] Win!
Put it together, yell!
Go—Fight—Win! Go—Fight—Win!

• • • • •

Jacket fans, help us out: yell, "Go!" [pause] Go!
Jacket fans, help us out: yell, "Fight!" [pause] Fight!
Jacket fans, help us out: yell, "Win!" [pause] Win!
Yell together: Go—Fight—Win!

• • • • •

Cava—lier Vic—tory!
Let's spell it out and start with V!
V—I—C—T—O—R—Y
Again! V—I—C—T—O—R—Y
One more time!
V—I—C—T—O—R—Y

• • • • •

Blue! [clap] Say it again! [pause] Blue!
Let's go!
White! [clap] Say it again! [pause] White!
Let's go!
Tigers! [clap] Say it again! Tigers!
Let's go!

• • • • •

G—O, G—O
Yell, "Go Green!" [pause] Go Green!
G—O, G—O
Yell, "Go Gold!" [pause] Go Gold!
Go Green! Go Gold! Go Green! Go Gold!

• • • • •

H! [clap—clap—clap] M! [clap—clap—clap] S! [clap—clap—clap]
H! [clap] M! [clap] S! [clap]
HMS! Go, Bears, go!

• • • • •

Fans in the stands, yell, "Let's go Blue!"
Let's go Blue!
Fans in the stands, yell, "Let's go Gold!"
Let's go Gold!
Let's go Blue! [pause] Let's go Gold!

Sidelines

D—D—Defense! [pause] Take that ball away!

• • • • •

T—A—K—E take that ball away!

• • • • •

H—O—L—D Hold that line!

• • • • •

Hands up! [clap—clap] Defense!

• • • • •

Push 'em! Push 'em back! Defense, push 'em hard!

• • • • •

Rebound! [pause] Pull it down! Go! [pause] Go! [pause] Go! [pause]

• • • • •

T—D! We want a touchdown!

• • • • •

Tighten up! Tighten up! Tighten up that line!

• • • • •

Take it away! [clap—clap] Take it away! [clap—clap]

• • • • •

Get that ball! Take it away!

• • • • •

1—2—3—4, Come on, Cats, let's score!

• • • • •

First 'n' 10, do it again, Go, Cardinals, go!

• • • • •

B—E—A—T, Come, Tigers, beat the Bears!

• • • • •

We are [clap—clap] Bull—dogs!

• • • • •

We want a touch—down [pause—pause] Hey, Tigers!

• • • • •

Score two, let's go, Bruins, Score two, let's go!

• • • • •

Hey, Hey! Here we go! Score, Cats, score!

•••••

Block that kick, Panthers, block that kick!

•••••

Go, go, Eagles! Heeey, go, Eagles!

•••••

G—O! Let's go, Tigers! G—O! Let's go!

•••••

Defense! Come on, defense! Hold that line!

•••••

What do we want? T—D! What's what? Touchdown!

•••••

Shove that ball across that line! Shove it! [pause—pause] Shove it!

•••••

Heeeeey, Tigers! Get! Fired! Up!

•••••

Come on, Panthers! We want two!

•••••

Touchdown! Touchdown! We want a Tiger touchdown!

•••••

De—fense! [clap—clap] De—fense! [clap—clap]

•••••

Here we go Ti—gers! Here we go! [clap—clap]

•••••

Shoot for two! [pause] Two! Two! [clap—clap—clap]

•••••

C—A—T—S! Cats! Cats! Cats!

•••••

Hold—'em! Panthers! Hold—'em! [clap—clap—clap]

•••••

Push—'em back! Push—'em back! Push—'em way back!

•••••

Here we go! Down the field! Score, Tigers, score!

About ASEP and Varsity Brands

Coaching Youth Cheerleading was cowritten by Varsity Brands and the American Sport Education Program (ASEP).

Varsity Brands was founded in 1974 and today trains more than 350,000 young people at various summer camps annually. As the largest cheerleading educational company in the world, Varsity Brands has helped to expand cheerleading's popularity through several educational entities including the Universal Cheerleaders Association (UCA) and the National Cheerleaders Association (NCA), and its ESPN televised national cheerleading championships. Varsity Brands is headquartered in Memphis, Tennessee.

ASEP has been developing and delivering coaching education courses since 1981. As the nation's leading coaching education program, ASEP works with national, state, and local youth sport organizations to develop educational programs for coaches, officials, administrators, and parents. These programs incorporate ASEP's philosophy of "Athletes first, winning second."